Tax Planning With Offshore Companies & Trusts

The A-Z Guide

Lee Hadnum LLB ACA CTA

WPR TAX PUBLISHING

Important Legal Notices

WealthProtectionReport™
Tax Planning With Offshore Companies & Trusts

Published by:

>WPR Tax Publishing
>BCB Bachstrasse 1
>CH-9606 Butschwil
>Switzerland

>email: sales@wealthprotectionreport.co.uk

First Edition, June 2013
ISBN 978-0-9576024-7-2

Copyright
Copyright © 2013 Lee Hadnum. All rights reserved.

No part of this publication may be reproduced or transmitted in any form or by any means (electronically or mechanically, including photocopying, recording or storing it in any medium by electronic means) without the prior permission in writing of the copyright owner except in accordance with the provisions of the Copyright, Designs and Patents Act 1988 or under the terms of a licence issued by the Copyright Licensing Agency Ltd, 90 Tottenham Court Road, London, W1P 0LP. All applications for the written permission of the copyright owner to reproduce or transmit any part of this Tax Guide should be sent to the publisher.

Warning: Any unauthorised reproduction or transmission of any part of this Tax Guide may result in criminal prosecution and a civil claim for damages.

Trademarks
The logo "WealthProtectionReport™" is a trademark of WealthProtectionReport.co.uk. All other logos, trademarks, names and logos in this Tax Guide may be trademarks of their respective owners.

Disclaimer
Before reading or relying on the content of this guide, please read the disclaimer carefully.

Disclaimer

1. Please note that this tax guide is intended as **general guidance only** for individual readers and does NOT constitute accountancy, tax, legal, investment or other professional advice. WealthProtectionReport and the author accept no responsibility or liability for loss which may arise from reliance on information contained in this tax guide.

2. Please note that tax legislation, the law and practices by government and regulatory authorities (for example, HM Revenue and Customs) are constantly changing and the information contained in this tax guide is only correct as at the date of publication. We therefore recommend that for accountancy, tax, investment or other professional advice, you consult a suitably qualified accountant, tax specialist, independent financial adviser, or other professional adviser. Please also note that your personal circumstances may vary from the general examples given in this tax guide and your professional adviser will be able to give specific advice based on your personal circumstances.

3. This tax guide covers UK taxation mainly and any references to 'tax' or 'taxation' in this tax guide, unless the contrary is expressly stated, are to UK taxation only. Please note that references to the 'UK' do not include the Channel Islands or the Isle of Man. Addressing all foreign tax implications is beyond the scope of this tax guide.

4. Whilst in an effort to be helpful, this tax guide may refer to general guidance on matters other than UK taxation, WealthProtectionReport and the author are not experts in these matters and do not accept any responsibility or liability for loss which may arise from reliance on such information contained in this tax guide.

Do you want more Information on offshore tax planning issues?

If you liked this tax guide and are interested in more tax articles and guidance from the author, Lee Hadnum, please visit:

www.wealthprotectionreport.co.uk

This is Lee's private membership site which provides subscribers with tax saving reports, articles, and advice.

Contents

Part I: Tax Planning With Offshore Companies

1. Introduction 3
2. Why Use An Offshore Company? 4
3. Types Of Offshore Entity 6
4. Making Sure The Company Is Non-Resident 13
5. A Look At The Anti Avoidance Rules 32
6. Reporting Income of An Offshore Company On UK Tax Returns 33
7. Apportionment Of Capital Gains 43
8. Who Can Use An Offshore Company Tax Efficiently? 50
9. Using An Offshore Holding Company For Non Doms 53
10. Overseas Trading 57
11. Controlled Foreign Companies 63
12. EU VAT Planning With An Offshore Structure 68
13. Trading In The UK With An Offshore Company 71
14. Tax Checklist: Using An Offshore Company 87

Part II: Tax Planning With Offshore Trusts

15. Introduction 93
16. How Offshore Trusts Are Taxed 94
17. The Offshore Trust Anti Avoidance Rules – Income Tax ... 99
18. The Offshore Trust Anti Avoidance Rules – Capital Gains Tax 106

19. Summary Of Tax Treatment For Offshore Trust/Beneficiaries 109

20. UK Protectors & Offshore Trusts 112

21. UK Tax For Offshore Life Interest Trusts 115

22. Migrating a UK Trust Overseas 118

23. Top Tax Planning Uses For Offshore Trusts 121

24. Using Offshore Trusts for CGT Avoidance 124

25. Offshore Trusts For Grandchildren 127

26. How Non Doms Can Use Offshore Trusts Even If They Don't Claim The Remittance Basis 129

27. How Non Doms Can Remit Income & Gains Tax Free With Offshore Trusts 132

28. Advanced Tax Planning For Non Doms Using Offshore Trusts To Purchase UK Property 135

29. UK Domiciliaries And Offshore Trusts 137

30. Using Offshore Trusts To Purchase Property 140

31. Getting Money Out of Offshore Trusts Tax Efficiently .. 146

32. Q & A's On Offshore Trusts 152

Appendix I: UK tax treatment of overseas entities 164

Part I
Tax Planning With Offshore Companies

Chapter 1

Introduction

If you're planning on using an offshore, non-resident company to reduce your UK taxes, there are some tremendous opportunities available.

However, it's not all plain sailing and you definitely need to consider some of the anti avoidance rules that HMRC have at their disposal to challenge your entitlement to these tax benefits.

The key rules that you'll need to be concerned with are:

- Establishing the top level management and control of the company as overseas

- Avoiding the income tax anti avoidance rules that can tax UK residents directly on the profits in the offshore company

- Avoiding the capital gains anti avoidance rules that can tax UK shareholders on capital gains in the offshore company

- Avoiding a UK trade, and in particular a UK permanent establishment as this can result in a UK tax charge even if the company is non-resident.

Some of these rules are being changed in the 2013 Finance Bill, although they apply retrospectively from April 2012;

We look at all of the above issues (and more) in this book.

Chapter 2

Why Use An Offshore Company?

This is the shortest chapter in the book, but one of the most important, as it focuses on the benefits of using an offshore company *if* you can get your tax planning right.

First though – what exactly is an offshore company?

Well for UK tax purposes, there's no real definition of a company as an "offshore company". What we're really talking about is any company that isn't UK resident. All non UK resident companies are subject to the same provisions. This applies whether they're based in traditional low tax jurisdictions such as the IOM, Channel Islands, the BVI etc., or whether they're based in other EU states (e.g. Spain, Germany etc.).

Of course this only applies to the UK treatment. The foreign taxes will be very different depending on your chosen jurisdiction.

Usually when we talk about offshore companies we're talking about a non-resident company that is based in a low tax jurisdiction. The idea being to avoid both UK and overseas taxes.

Purely from a UK perspective though, providing a company is non-resident it can gain some good tax advantages.

UK residence

A UK resident company is subject to UK corporation tax on its worldwide income and gains. By contrast a non-UK resident company is only subject to corporation tax on its UK income.

At first glance, therefore, it would seem that an offshore company is an effective way of sheltering income and capital gains from the taxman, as all foreign income and gains accruing to the company should be free of UK tax.

In fact using a *directly owned* offshore company is not a straightforward option to avoid UK taxes. One of the reasons for this is the issue of 'deemed' company residence. A company is regarded as a UK resident if:

- It is a UK incorporated company, or
- Its *central management and control* is in the UK.

We'll look at this shortly, but assuming you can arrange the structuring correctly the potential advantage is huge.

If you can establish a company as non-UK resident it will be:

- Exempt from tax on capital gains (providing the assets aren't used for the purpose of a UK trade or the company is selling UK residential property valued at more than £2 Million.
- Exempt from tax on all foreign profits

Only UK trading profits would remain subject to UK tax, however even then it's usually required that there is a UK permanent establishment before there can be a UK tax charge.

This means that anyone carrying out an overseas trade or who is an investor could see significant tax advantages from using a non UK company.

The first step in obtaining this tax free trading/investment is to use an overseas company that is managed and controlled from overseas.

Chapter 3

Types Of Offshore Entity

When looking at the various options available to you to structure your affairs you'll find that there are a number of different entities – both onshore and offshore – that can be used. It can be difficult to understand the differences between the various options so we'll look briefly at each.

UK Limited Company (Ltd)

This is your bog standard company used by traders and investors. It can be used to hold pretty much all assets and can carry out most activities.

When you form the company you'll need to provide some details to both Companies House and later HMRC. Note that any UK incorporated company is automatically classed as UK resident and is therefore taxed in the UK on its worldwide income.

UK Ltd companies are very cheap to form and ongoing administration is not too onerous. You'll need to file annual accounts in a suitable format, and also submit the annual return (which contains details of the company and shareholders).

In terms of asset protection it can be a good way to hold assets separately although, as we've seen, the courts can ignore the company where the arrangement looks like a sham, so you'll need to ensure that there is commercial substance.

If you're looking to trade overseas, a UK company has the advantage of looking highly professional and would not draw attention to your activities, unlike companies registered in certain tax havens. Therefore using a UK Ltd nominee company is popular, to combine a professional front with minimising taxes.

The Ltd company is a separate entity from its shareholders. It can therefore sue or be sued in its own name and will be treated for tax purposes separately from its directors and shareholders. One of the main purposes of forming a Ltd. company can be to minimise UK taxes.

UK companies pay UK corporation tax as opposed to UK income tax and for most this will mean paying corporation tax at 20% as opposed to 40% income tax. Provided only limited profits are then extracted from the company (for example, only enough to use up the basic-rate tax band) there would be no further tax to pay.

You won't be able to establish this company as non-resident (as it's UK incorporated), therefore if you want to trade overseas and take advantage of the tax exemption for non-resident companies you'd need to use a different company.

UK Limited Liability Partnership (LLP)

This is a cross between a Ltd. company and a normal partnership. It was primarily introduced for the large professional firms that carried on a trade as a partnership (for example, lawyers, accountants and surveyors) but who wanted the benefit of limited liability protection.

Therefore an LLP allows the members to protect their personal assets from any creditors, but for tax purposes it is treated just like any other partnership. The LLP will be taxed on a 'pass through' basis with each partner being treated as owning a share in the partnership assets. The profits of the partnership would then be attributed to the partners, irrespective of whether the partners actually take their share of the profits out of the partnership or not.

For asset protection purposes it offers pretty much the same protection as a Ltd. company. In tax terms the tax liability will depend on the partners' residence and other taxable income.

If an LLP is used with a mixture of UK and overseas partners, it would be only the UK partners that would be taxed in the UK, with the overseas partners being taxed in their country of residence. Where there are mixed residence partnerships an LLP may therefore be preferred to a UK company.

International Business Company (IBC)

This is the name typically given to an offshore company that has been formed outside the UK.

There are three main reasons that an IBC may be used.

- To avoid UK taxes

- To hide assets

- To trade overseas, either by UK or overseas residents.

Rather than using a simple offshore bank account, many people use an offshore account with the account holder being an IBC – the aim being to sever the link between the individual and the offshore assets.

As with UK companies, IBCs can be used for practically any purpose, including holding overseas property and shares, bank accounts and other assets.

Unlike UK companies, an IBC usually has much lower disclosure requirements with hardly any form filling, no annual accounts or returns and no annual general meeting. It's usually also exempt from local taxes provided you incorporate in a suitable jurisdiction.

Bearer Share Companies

There are a number of jurisdictions (such as the British Virgin Islands) that permit you to form a special bearer share company. This will cost you more than a standard company – but what benefit do you get for the extra cash?

A normal company lists the owner of the shares on the share certificates and when you want to transfer ownership of the shares you need to notify Companies House.

A bearer share company is totally different. The owner of the company is the person who happens to be holding the share certificate. This means that, provided you do not have the bearer certificates in your possession, you can state that you don't legally own a particular company.

Note the company will still need to pay tax on any profits generated. The only real benefit is in terms of privacy. It would make it more difficult for anyone to argue that you owned a company if bearer shares were used.

Limited Liability Company (LLC)

LLCs are available in a number of jurisdictions, although it has to be said that United States LLCs (in particular the Delaware LLC) are the most popular. The LLC is similar to the UK LLP, although there are some important differences.

An LLC is a cross between the UK's LLP and a company. Unlike an LLP an LLC is taxed as a separate entity in many jurisdictions and would therefore be subject to corporation tax on its profits.

Individuals who own an interest in an LLC are known as 'members' as opposed to shareholders.

The LLC structure is known to be very flexible and, in particular, documentary requirements are pretty slack with few requirements to keep minutes or have records of formal resolutions.

It also benefits from limited liability, thus ensuring that your personal assets are kept separate from your business assets.

Unlike an LLP, the minimum number of people needed to form an LLC is one, with a few exceptions. If you did incorporate it with just one member, this would be akin to a one man limited company, albeit with low disclosure and documentary requirements.

Trusts

Trusts were traditionally one of the most popular entities for holding assets. They were particularly useful as they allowed an individual to legally give away assets but still exercise an element of control over them (as a trustee) and in some cases benefit from the assets (as a beneficiary).

In terms of avoiding UK taxes they are much less attractive now than they used to be due to the number of anti-avoidance provisions that operate to negate the tax benefits.

Offshore trusts would usually be used in combination with another entity such as an IBC or a foundation. Typically the trust would be used to hold the shares of an IBC. Alternatively, if a foundation structure was used, the trust could be the beneficiary of the foundation.

Foundations

The use of a foundation has gained in popularity over the past few years, given its unique characteristics. The foundation is essentially a cross between a trust and a company because it's a separate legal entity that doesn't have owners.

Foundations are useful because they have a separate legal personality. Therefore when applying for an offshore bank account, it is often necessary to state the beneficial owners. If a foundation is used it is the foundation itself that is the beneficial owner. Foundations are popular primarily for asset protection purposes.

In UK tax terms, they'd be treated in a similar way to a company.

Protected Cell Companies (PCCs)

Protected cell companies are something of a new development. There are very few jurisdictions that permit them (including Guernsey, Bermuda and Mauritius) and although aimed at big business and the structuring of finance for multinational companies, they could be tailored to a smaller operation if required.

A protected cell company is a company that is split up into different sections. Each section is separate from all the others and rather than simply transferring assets to the company, you transfer assets to the particular cell of the company. Each cell is independent and separate from every other cell.

Therefore, rather than holding assets in separate companies, you could establish one PCC and put different assets in each cell. In terms of any creditors each cell would need to be approached separately and the assets of one cell could not be used to satisfy liabilities of another cell.

They're principally asset protection tools and, given the right circumstances, for example if there is a diverse range of assets involved, they could be useful.

How overseas entities are treated by the UK authorities

If you're planning on using an overseas trust or company it is essential to ensure that you know exactly how it will be treated by the UK taxman.

There are broadly speaking two ways in which an overseas entity could be classed. It could either be classed like a UK partnership or LLP (known as 'transparent') or like a UK limited liability company (known as 'Opaque').

The difference is crucial, as it will impact directly on how any overseas profits are taxed in the UK.

A transparent entity such as an LLP or a partnership is taxed directly on the members. In other words the members are treated as earning the profits in their name and therefore any profits that a transparent entity makes are taxed on the members, irrespective of whether the profits are actually paid out to the members.

An Opaque entity is treated as earning the profits in its name. Therefore the members are only taxed on the amounts they actually extract from the company.

In order to decide whether an overseas entity is transparent or opaque there are a number of tests that the UK tax authorities will look at. In particular, they will look at the following:

- Does the overseas entity have a separate legal existence?

- Does the entity issue share capital or something that is similar to share capital?

- Is the business carried on by the entity itself or by the members who have an interest in it?

- Are the members entitled to share in the entities profits as they arise or does the amount of profits to which they are entitled depend on a decision of the entity or its members (e.g. in a UK company where the dividend needs to be declared by directors)

- Who is responsible for any business debts - the entity or the members?

- Do the entities assets belong to the entity or to the members?

Of key importance will be the impact of foreign law and in particular they will look at the distribution of profits from the entity and who actually carries out the business.

Essentially it's a case of looking at where the true rights of ownership and control arise. However, rather than assessing each overseas entity from scratch the UK taxman has previously looked at a number of foreign entities to assess their UK treatment. Whilst this should be regarded as a general overview only, I've highlighted the UK treatment in appendix I.

Therefore if you're considering using an offshore entity it's well worth checking whether based on the above issues it will be taxed as an opaque or transparent entity.

Chapter 4

Making Sure The Company Is Non-Resident

Establishing a company as non-resident is now mainly applicable to offshore/overseas companies that can establish their management and control overseas.

If you can do this, the company will be non-resident and exempt from UK tax on overseas income and capital gains.

However actually achieving this is less straightforward.

HMRC has stated that it will look at offshore companies to identify if there has been an attempt to create simply the appearance of central management and control in a place.

Therefore, care is needed to ensure that any overseas directors are actually running the company.

It's essentially a question of fact so HMRC/the Commissioners will look at where in actual fact the company is controlled from (where the 'real heart' of the company is). However when they refer to 'management and control' exactly what level of control do they mean?

Company Command Structure

HMRC split a company's management into three different levels:

Level 1

This is the shop floor management. So in the case of a shop for instance you may have the shop manager or the supervisor.

Level 2

This is the head office or the place where the executives and senior managers are. This is where the company's operations are controlled from and where the orders are given.

Level 3

This is referred to by HMRC as the 'central policy core of the whole enterprise'. This is where the long term strategy and operations are governed from. This could be an active or a passive body.

You'll probably have realised that there will often be no clearly definable split between the three levels.

In a small enterprise for instance you could have all 3 levels in the same person.

Similarly you may find that in many small companies level 2 is effectively the same as level 3. So if you have a small company which runs 5 restaurants the individual restaurant managers would represent level 1. The head office could be run by the directors who together represent the board. If all the directors are UK residents who actually live and work in the UK they would represent the level 2 and level 3.

It is however the level 3 control that is of key importance for establishing non-residence.

How to establish level 3 overseas

In the past there used to be more of a clearly definable split between levels 2 and 3.

In the case of the restaurant business above you may have had the head office run by a general manager and a team of senior managers. They would not be board members.

The board would have been primarily non-executive directors who

TAX PLANNING WITH OFFSHORE COMPANIES & TRUSTS | 15

exercised the active control over the senior managers. It was the non-execs that would have represented the level 3 management.

Now, the usual practice is for executive directors to actually exercise some element of control.

A common scenario is to use nominee directors based overseas to act as the board.

The problem you have is that there is no written law that the board of directors represents the level 3 management. In various cases the courts have affirmed that the constitutional position based on company law is not definitive. It's always a question of fact.

So if you lived and worked in the UK but actually directed the nominee directors you would represent the level 3 management in the company. The board would need to actually have independent authority and actually exercise it on occasion (even if it was passive for long periods).

Nevertheless in most cases where there is a board that is actively controlling the company this is where the level 3 control will be.

So how does this impact on you looking to establish level 3 management overseas?

We'll look at this in detail shortly, but some options to consider could be:

- Establish an overseas board with both executive and non- executive directors. The executive directors may be based in the UK but the non-execs could be overseas. Having overseas non-execs may be preferable to having overseas execs. You would though need to ensure that they actually exercised control and actively intervened in the working of the company.

- Having an MD or Chief Executive based overseas with near sole power. We look at this again shortly.

What is in your favour though is that whilst level 2 management may be relatively difficult to transfer overseas, level 3 is much less so as the board does not have to be tied to the operational base.

HMRC provide a concise example which highlights the key points well:

'...A small grocery store is run by a man A and his son A junior. There is a grandfather, once sole proprietor, who no longer takes an active part in the business but owns the property and makes his views known on important matters. A company is formed with A as chairman and managing director, the son as sales director and grandfather as a mere shareholder.

Every year A and his son spend holidays in Jersey. It is very unlikely that any body of Commissioners would accept that by holding their only board meetings when they are in Jersey they had made the company resident outside the United Kingdom. Both level two and level three management are exercised by A and his son and they are clearly based in the United Kingdom.

But an alternative scenario has grandfather as both major shareholder and chairman with A and his son as full-time working directors. Grandfather takes no part in the day-to-day running of the business but takes a keen interest in its success and his word on important matters carries great weight.

Here level three management emerges as something quite distinct from level two which remains with A and his son. Level three may be found either with grandfather alone or with grandfather and his sons acting as a board depending on the extent of grandfather's real power. If grandfather moves to Jersey, level three management may genuinely move with him, either because he alone exercises central management and control from Jersey or because the board meetings, at which he plays an important part, are held there...'

This example shows nicely how the level 3 management is crucial. You can appoint an overseas MD, Chairman or other senior figure who has overall control and have the level 2 in the UK. You can do this by ensuring that either:

- the senior figure exercised sole level 3 control or
- the senior figure and UK directors exercised control at the board level and board meetings are based overseas.

The senior figure in this case is essentially acting in a similar role to the-non execs who would have previously kept a close eye on the other directors.

Note though that the position as a shareholder is only relevant to the issue of control if the directors actually stand aside and are directed by the shareholders (as in this case they would exercise the level 3 control).

Review of HMRC draft guidance on company non-residence

HMRC have recently published some draft guidance on when they will and won't enquire into a company's residence status. In this section we provide a brief overview of the impact of this guidance.

Circumstances in which HMRC will not usually review residence - limitations

HMRC provide a number of examples when they won't look to argue that a foreign company is UK resident.

For all examples they assume that:

- the company is wholly owned by a UK headed group or a UK headed sub-group with a non-UK resident ultimate parent;

- the company is incorporated outside of the UK in a territory where it is considered to be resident for tax purposes by virtue of its incorporation there;

- the country of incorporation and residence has a double taxation agreement with the UK which contains a residence tie-breaker

- the company is genuinely established in its territory of residence;

- the company does not (except in the particular circumstances of examples 6 to 8) have investment business as its main business, and;

- the central management and control of the business of the company is at least in part exercised at meetings of its board of directors.

Example 1

A company includes as a member of its board of directors a UK resident, all other members being resident in its territory of residence and elsewhere outside of the UK. The company's board of directors meets only outside of the UK.

Example 2

A company has more than one UK based director on its board, but the majority of board members are based outside of the UK in its territory of residence or elsewhere. The board meets only outside of the UK.

Example 3

The minority UK based attendance in example 2 becomes a majority on an isolated occasion due to the unforeseen unavailability of one or more of the overseas based directors.

Example 4

The UK based directors in examples 1 and 2 do not travel to attend board meetings in person but habitually participate by electronic link from the UK.

Example 5

The board of directors in examples 1 and 2 hold the majority of its meetings in any one accounting period outside of the UK but a small minority -- no more than one or two -- of the meetings are habitually held in the UK.

Example 6

A company has as its main business the holding of majority shareholdings in operating companies resident in its own territory of residence or region (which does not include the UK). Its board of directors meets both in its territory of incorporation and in the territories of incorporation of its subsidiaries. It includes on its board a minority of one or more UK based directors.

Example 7

The UK based directors in example 6 habitually participate in meetings by way of electronic link from the UK.

Example 8

The situation is the same as in examples 6 or 7 except that while the board holds the majority of its meetings in any one accounting period outside of the UK, a small minority of the meetings (no more than one or two) are habitually held in the UK.

Example 9

The majority of directors habitually perform a significant part of their duties in the UK, merely leaving the UK to attend board meetings. HMRC may wish to examine all relevant factors in such a case to determine whether or not the company should be regarded as resident in the UK.

There will be lots of cases that fall outside these examples (e.g. where the company is not owned by a UK headed group or sub group). You would need to assess whether they have a huge impact on the position as outlined above.

A couple of points that are worth stating are:

- HMRC have stated that it's not the number of UK meetings v the number of overseas meetings that is important. Rather it is what happened at particular board meetings and what happened between them
- Also the location of a Director's tax residence doesn't impact on the residence of the company. Instead it is the location where the management and control are carried out that is important (not necessarily the same as the country of tax residence).

Cases on company residence

There have been a couple of important appeals, heard by the Upper Tribunal/the Courts which relate to company residence.

It's worthwhile reviewing these as they provide some interesting insights into how the Courts approach questions of overseas company residence.

The first was the Laerstate BV appeal.

Laerstate BV

In the original decision the company was unsuccessful in arguing that it was non-resident. However it did set out the various tests to be applied in determining corporate residence.

Having regard to the importance of the subject matter, and the fact that the taxpayer's appeal to the Upper Tribunal has been struck out, it may be helpful to repeat the substance of the Tribunal's comments:

- There remains the classic formulation that a company resides where its real business is carried on - where the central management and control actually abides.

- There is no assumption that central management and control must be found where the directors meet. Where a company is managed by its directors in board meetings, that may be the location of central management and control. But if the management is carried out outside board meetings, it is necessary to identify who is managing the company and making the high-level decisions - and where they were doing it. (This remains the case, even though it may be contrary to the company's constitution.)

- The whole picture must be considered to arrive at the factual conclusion of where central management and control abides. The location of the signing of documents and the making of board resolutions is significant, but a company's residence will not fluctuate merely because individual acts of management take place in different places.

- The mere act of signing documents is not conclusive - the local directors must apply their minds to whether or not to sign the documents. There is nothing to prevent a majority shareholder from indicating how the directors of the company should act.

   If the directors consider those wishes and act on them, it is still their decision. The distinction is between directors making a decision and not a making decision at all - for example, just signing documents without any real consideration. The decisions of the directors must be informed decisions - merely going through the motions is not enough. The directors might follow the wishes of the shareholders, but they must have the minimum information necessary to make a decision. Without that minimum information, there will be no decision at all.

- It would be exceptional for a parent company to assume the functional management of its subsidiary; a parent usually operates through the boards of its subsidiaries.

However, this would not be the case if the parent company usurps the functions of the local boards.

Smallwood Decision

Mr Smallwood, a U.K. resident, decided that a Jersey Trust of which he was the settlor, and in which he maintained an interest, should dispose of certain shares. He obtained advice from accountants that if the trust sold the shares the gain would be attributed to him because of a provision in the taxing statute that would apply "if the trustees were not resident in the UK during any part of the year". The Bristol advisors then informed Mr. Smallwood that there was an off-the-peg "Round the World" tax scheme that was intended to eliminate the tax.

How the round the world scheme worked

In implementing the RTW scheme, the Jersey trustee was replaced with a Mauritius trustee, and the Mauritius trustee was in turn replaced by Mr. and Mrs. Smallwood as trustees in March 2001, prior to the April 5 tax year-end of the trust under U.K. tax law.

The intention was that when the shares were sold during January of 2001 the trust's capital gain would be protected from U.K. tax by virtue of the provisions of the U.K.-Mauritius Tax Treaty. Further, as Mr. and Mrs. Smallwood, being U.K. residents, would be trustees "for part of the year" the attribution rule would not apply and no tax would be payable on the gain in the U.K.

The Appeal decision

The primary question was whether the Treaty applied to exempt the trust's gain from U.K. tax. The threshold issue was whether the matter of residence fell to be determined at the date of the disposal or more generally within the year of the disposition. Clearly the trust was, at least, resident in the U.K. from March 2 until April 5.

On July 8, 2010, the Court of Appeal held in HMRC v. Smallwood & Anor, that the issue of whether the taxpayer should be resident in a particular state at the time of disposal or at some other point in time is an issue for each state to decide as part of its own taxation regime. The Treaty must be assumed to have been drafted in a way that contemplates any tax treatment of capital gains based on residence or similar criteria.

"Resident of a contracting state" means chargeable to tax in that state on account of residence and, for this purpose, one has to take into account the tax treatment of the gain under the domestic legislation of both contracting states regardless of the period of residence which gives rise to the liability. The Treaty accommodates legislation under which a gain is made taxable in the U.K. by virtue of residence in a period after the gain has occurred.

Place of effective management/central management and control

The Court concluded that the trust was resident in both Mauritius and the U.K. under each jurisdiction's domestic legislation. The issue then fell to be determined under the tie-breaker rule in the Treaty based on the place of effective management ("POEM"). The judges stated that it was difficult to draw any distinction between the concepts of POEM and central management and control ("CMC"), the later being the terminology generally used to describe the test in cases dealing with the residence of companies.

The Court referred to the OECD commentary on Article 4(3) of the Model Convention, which provides that "the POEM is the place where key management and commercial decisions that are necessary for the conduct of the entity's business are in substance made. An entity may have more than one place of management, but it can only have one place of effective management at any one time." What has to be identified is the place where the real top-level management of the trustee occurred rather than day-to-day administration of the trust.

It was found as a fact by the Special Commissioners that the appropriate meetings took place in Mauritius and the necessary resolutions were passed in Mauritius by the Mauritius trustee.

The books and records were properly maintained. While there was a "confident expectation" that the Mauritius trustee would choose to sell the shares, there was no agreement that the trustee would behave in a certain way or would make certain decisions. Its duties as a trustee were laid down in the legislation.

If it had not been in the interest of the beneficiaries, the trustee would not have sold the shares. For example, if the share price dropped dramatically, and if the fund manager had advised against the sale, then the trustee would have decided not to sell.

However, the facts surrounding the appointment of the Mauritius trustee led the Court to conclude that the real top level management, or the realistic, positive management of the trust, remained in the United Kingdom.

The sale of the shares was motivated by U.K. tax planning reasons.

The details relating to the actual sales were found to be low level management decisions, as there was no doubt the shares would be sold; the real top level management decisions or the realistic, positive management decisions of the trust, to dispose of all the shares in a tax efficient way, had already been, and continued to be, taken in the United Kingdom. Mr. Smallwood had the power to appoint new trustees.

The Court adopted a two-prong test in deciding where POEM or CMC resides.

The first question is whether:

(i) CMC is exercised through the constitutional organs of the vehicle in question, or

(ii) the functions of those constitutional organs are usurped.

If the functions have not been usurped, the test requires that a second question be asked, namely whether there is an "outsider" that

(iii) proposes, advises and influences the decisions which the constitutional organs take in fulfilling their functions, or

(iv) dictates the decisions which are to be taken.

If either (ii) or (iv) occurs, POEM or CMC will generally reside where the usurper or outsider makes its decisions.

In Smallwood, the POEM test inevitably led to the question of whether the effective decision by the Mauritius trustees to sell the shares was taken by the Board of Directors of the trustee (albeit on the advice of, and at the request of, the U.K. advisers), or whether the Mauritius trustee effectively ceded any discretion in the matter to the U.K. advisors by agreeing to act in accordance with their instructions.

The majority of the Court agreed that the POEM of the Mauritius trustee and of the trust was in the U.K. There was a scheme of management of this trust which went above and beyond the day-to-day management exercised by the trustee for the time being, and the control of it was located in the United Kingdom.

Conclusion

This case remains a useful reminder of the issues in establishing central and management control overseas in the context of an offshore company.

In particular the confirmation that you need to look at (1) whether there has been a usurping of the Directors' powers, and if not (ii) whether there is an external party that dictates decisions to the Directors is useful. As always the emphasis is on the top level "real management" (or the "level 3" management) of the company, rather than the lower level management being overseas as was the case here.

Best practice guidelines to establish company as non-resident

OK, so having taken all of the above into account, how do you go about ensuring that your company is non-resident?

If you want to be able to clearly establish as being non-resident some of the best practice recommendations to establish this include:

1. Board meetings

- A majority (as a minimum, but preferably all) of the directors of the offshore company should be resident for tax purposes outside the UK, preferably in the relevant offshore jurisdiction.

- Regular board meetings should be held outside the UK, preferably in the relevant offshore jurisdiction. Detailed minutes of board meetings should be made and kept securely. Directors should attend board meetings ideally in person and certainly not by telephone from the UK.

- Directors should be suitably qualified and have relevant experience for the business undertaken by the offshore company. They should all be fully aware of the business operations of the company and, as a result, be able to ask relevant, pertinent questions regarding the business tabled at board meetings so that informed decisions can be made.

- The directors should be familiar with the constitutional documents of the company and in particular any investment restrictions. Service provider contracts with the company should have reasonable terms and be properly performed and monitored.

- Strategic decisions should only be made following due consideration by the directors at a properly convened board meeting.

2. Documents

- The directors should be provided with full information, and in sufficient time, to allow them to make a considered decision about the matters to be discussed at board meetings. It is important for the directors to duly consider all matters tabled at a board meeting, investigate any concerns, and be seen properly to exercise their power. Board meetings should not simply "rubber stamp" proposals put forward by any UK resident managers or executives of a UK resident parent company.

- Consider carefully the governing law of the key documents to be executed by the offshore company. If it is English law, then consider whether or not that is appropriate in the circumstances. There could be good reason, in certain cases, for English law to apply. If, however, there are no UK resident parties to a document then consider whether the governing law of a different jurisdiction would be more appropriate.

- Ensure that emails and other communications made by fund managers and advisers to the offshore company are properly directed to the managers or executives of the company rather than exclusively to individuals resident in the UK.

- A copy of all documents involving the offshore company should be kept by the company at its registered office or principal place of business in the jurisdiction concerned.

3. Execution of agreements

- Once written agreements have been duly considered and approved by the board of the offshore company, it is preferable for such agreements to be signed by non-UK resident directors rather than signed in the UK by any UK resident directors.

- It is more important, however, that the actual decision to execute is made in the relevant offshore jurisdiction, rather than the manner of execution of that decision. HM Revenue & Customers (HMRC) recognises in its guidance notes that "the mere physical acts of signing resolutions or documents does not suffice for actual management".

4. UK resident parent company

- Care is required in any dealings between a UK resident parent company and its offshore subsidiary. HMRC recognises that it is particularly difficult to apply the central management and control (CMC) test when the offshore company has a UK-based parent. It is expected that the parent company will usually influence the activities of its subsidiary, especially if it is the sole or majority shareholder.

- It is acceptable for the parent company to exercise those powers that are typically reserved for a shareholder, such as the appointment and removal of directors, and approving the financial structure of a subsidiary. HMRC confirms in its guidance that it would not usually seek to argue, in these cases, that the CMC of the subsidiary is in the UK.

- The situation differs however, when the parent company usurps the function of the subsidiary's board, or where the board simply rubber stamps the parent company's decisions without giving independent consideration to the same. In these instances, HMRC will draw the conclusion that the subsidiary is subject to CMC from the UK and is therefore UK resident for tax purposes.

5. Delegation of decisions to the UK resident management company

- Great care is also needed when an offshore company delegates certain decisions to a UK resident company or other agent. What decisions can be delegated without prejudicing the offshore company's tax residence? HMRC acknowledges that it is possible to delegate certain decisions to a UK agent without necessarily bringing the offshore company within the territorial scope of UK tax. HMRC considers that offshore companies: "can exercise power in truth and fact by doing very little indeed. They can appoint agents and servants to attend to the day-to-day running of affairs..."

HMRC's guidance, and the relevant case law, can be difficult to interpret and apply in practice. While it seems clear that the key strategic decisions of a company should be taken by the board, and that the more routine day-to-day decisions could be delegated, what about the decisions which fall between the two?

In practice we have seen the following methods used to try to facilitate the identification of decisions which can be safely delegated:

1. By listing the broad type of decisions that the offshore company will face in practice and separating out the important strategic decisions from a list of the more routine day-to-day decisions.

    Examples of key strategic decisions are: the acquisition or disposal of material assets (including real estate or shares in other companies); the approval of annual accounts and tax returns; financial decisions (borrowing and calling down contributions from shareholders); and adopting the annual business plan and budget. Examples of routine day-to-day decisions are: collecting rent and service charges; and undertaking routine maintenance. Such day-to-day decisions can usually be delegated to a UK resident asset manager.

2. By reference to the business plan and budget adopted by the offshore company's board. Decisions relating to the implementation of matters approved in the business plan or budget may be delegated. This delegation may also (and should) be subject to additional parameters

set by the offshore company's board. Any items of expenditure not specifically referred to in the approved budget or business plan must be referred to the offshore company's board before being expended.

3. By reference to an appropriate financial threshold. The board of the offshore company may decide that certain decisions that fall below a certain financial threshold are of less strategic importance and hence can be delegated. The threshold needs to be carefully considered and selected by the board.

4. If any delegation is to be agreed, then the terms should be set out clearly in a written agreement. The terms of the delegated authority should be fully and carefully considered by the board of the offshore company before it is executed (and in accordance with the recommendations above).

Typical questions in an enquiry into the residence of an offshore company

As we've seen if you're planning on setting up an offshore company to avoid UK corporation tax on the profits of a UK trade or capital gains, one of the difficulties is ensuring that the central management and control is based overseas.

Below we've listed some of the questions that HMRC may raise in an enquiry into the residence of an offshore company:

- Please let me have copies of the minutes of the board meetings of the company.

- Please may I have the addresses of the directors of the offshore company?

- Where did the board meetings take place if not in the country of incorporation?

- Please provide an analysis of general and administrative costs of the company in reasonable detail.

- Does the company have any clerical support? If so, from whom is it provided?

- What services did the UK resident Directors provide to the company and where did they provide them?

- Please provide copies of the contracts of employment of the directors of the offshore company together with details of hours worked and responsibilities. Why is the remuneration of the directors so low when they apparently have responsibility for a company holding assets worth X millions of pounds?

- Please provide an analysis of professional fees stating who these were paid to and for what?

- Please let me have a detailed analysis of the telephone bills of the offshore company for the year.

- Please let me have a detailed analysis of business trips undertaken by the directors of the company during the period under review.

- Please may I have copies of all purchase and sale agreements entered into by the offshore company? Who made the decision that the purchases would be made?

- Who is legally entrusted to exercise central management and control and where is this duty carried out and when?

- Who makes the strategic decisions relating to the company, e.g. in respect of acquisitions etc.?

- Please may I have copies of the documentation of those decisions? Where were they taken?

- Does the company have a bank account? If so, where is it held and who has the right to draw? Are these rights to draw subject to any conditions or counter signatures?

- Where is the rest of the business of the company carried on?

- Who approves lines of bank credit for the company? Who authorises which bank and financial institutions are to be used as the company's depository and please let me have copies of documented decisions.

- Who approves capital expenditure and capital projects? Please let me have copies of the documented decisions.

- Who approves audited accounts and where?

You'll see from these questions that they cover the types of issues we've raised above. In particular ensuring that the strategic control overseas is real and that the overseas board of directors is not just acting on behalf of the UK shareholders. Particular care needs to be taken with documentation to support this, including the minutes of board meetings.

Chapter 5

A Look At The Anti Avoidance Rules

Although establishing the company as non-resident means the company itself won't be taxed on foreign income (and most capital gains), it doesn't mean that its tax efficient.

The UK has a number of anti avoidance rules that apply to non- resident companies. The aim of these is to withdraw the tax advantages offered by offshore companies in various circumstances.

They do this by taxing UK resident shareholders and other "beneficiaries" on the income and gains of the offshore company.

The main rules that you need to be concerned with are:

- The transfer of asset provisions that tax UK residents on overseas income arising to the offshore company
- The attribution rules that tax capital gains on UK shareholders of the offshore company.

Both of these are being significantly changed as a result of provisions in the 2013 Finance Bill.

We take a look at these rules in the next two chapters.

Chapter 6

Reporting Income of An Offshore Company On UK Tax Returns

How do the anti avoidance rules work?

The key provisions are in S720-731 ITA 2007, which provide for wide-ranging anti-avoidance powers designed to prevent the avoidance of Income Tax by individuals using offshore companies (and trusts).

The conditions for application of Section 720 and S727 are:

- There must be a transfer of assets by an individual
- As a result of the transfer income becomes payable to a non-resident person.
- The transferor must have power to enjoy that income in some way, or receive/be entitled to receive a capital sum.
- The transferor must be ordinarily resident in the UK in the year of liability.

If all of these conditions are fulfilled, the income which becomes payable to the offshore company is deemed to be that of the individual who made the transfer, to the extent he has power to enjoy that income.

The first point to consider would be whether there would be a 'transfer of assets' by you. The UK tax authorities take a wide view of what constitutes a transfer of assets.

For example S720 may apply:

- where an individual transfers cash to establish a non- resident trust, or
- subscribes for the share capital of an offshore company, or
- where an individual transfers assets such as shares or property to a new or existing non-resident trust or other company abroad.

It can also apply where intangible assets are transferred; for example a UK individual may transfer his services to an offshore company.

The view of the Revenue is that a transfer may be made by way of sale or purchase of assets, or by way of gift.

On the basis that the conditions above were satisfied, any income arising to the non-resident company can be taxed by S720, whether UK source income or foreign source income.

Note that one of the above conditions is that the UK resident must have power to enjoy the income arising to the non-resident (e.g. as a shareholder of an overseas company). Even if you did not actually receive any income from the company it is the potential to enjoy the income that is important. As such you would not have to actually receive any of the income at all.

Any income of the offshore company that was taxed on you would go in the foreign pages of the tax return here:

A Country or territory code	B Amount of income arising or received before any tax taken off	C Foreign tax taken off or paid

All other income received by a person abroad and any remitted 'ring fenced' foreign income - *read Helpsheet 262 if you are omitting income from this section because you are claiming an exemption, see box 46*

The alternative provision is S731.

This applies where assets have been transferred abroad and a UK resident other than the settlor obtains a benefit. In order for this to apply the following conditions would need to be satisfied:

- There must be a transfer of assets.
- As a result of which (alone or in conjunction with associated operations) income becomes payable to a non-resident person.
- As a result of the transfer, an individual other than the transferor receives a benefit, which is not otherwise chargeable to Income Tax.

- The recipient of the benefit must be ordinarily resident in the UK in the year of charge.

Section 731 is different from S720 in that it taxes non-transferors on benefits received.

Benefits chargeable by Section 731 include payments of any kind, for example cash (capital distributions), the use of property (e.g. rent free occupation of a house), interest free loans, etc.

Where the conditions are satisfied, the individual receiving the benefit is liable to tax on the amount or value of the benefit, (although the charge can be limited by the amount of past or future available 'relevant income' of the trust - see below).

It's also worth bearing in mind that Section 731 charges the amount or value of the benefit received to the extent that it is matched by the available relevant income of the offshore trust or company. This means any income which arises to the offshore company and which, as a result of the transfer can be used directly or indirectly for providing a benefit for the beneficiary. As such if the company had no income there may be no tax charge under S731.

You would declare any benefits taxable under S731 in box 42 of the foreign pages :

---

42 **If you have received a benefit from a person abroad, enter the value or payment received** – *if you are omitting income from this section because you are claiming an exemption, see box 46*

£ ☐☐☐☐☐☐☐

Even if there is a liability under S720 -- S731 what impact would this have?

Where the provisions apply this would deem the income or benefit to arise to the UK individual and would therefore be subject to UK income tax. S720-S731 applies unless you can show that the exemption in S733 onwards applies.

Motive Exemption

If you qualify for the motive exemption this can completely eliminate any income tax charges that would ordinarily apply under the above provisions.

In order for this to apply you would need to demonstrate either condition A or condition B is satisfied:

Condition A

It would not be reasonable to draw the conclusion, from all the circumstances of the case, that the purpose of avoiding liability to taxation was the purpose, or one of the purposes, for which the relevant transactions or any of them were effected.

Condition B

All the relevant transactions were genuine commercial transactions. It would not be reasonable to draw the conclusion, from all the circumstances of the case, that any one or more of those transactions was more than incidentally designed for the purpose of avoiding liability to taxation.

Actually persuading the Revenue that you can take advantage of this exemption can in practice be difficult.

So who can take advantage of the motive exemption?

The main cases where you'll be able to take advantage of the motive exemption are:

- Where you carry on a business abroad. Provided the reason for the use of an offshore company is commercial you'll be able to claim exemption from the income tax avoidance rules.

So you'd be looking at any arguments that support your requirement to use an local company (e.g. for commercial purposes having a locally incorporated company may be preferred by customers etc.).

- Where the offshore company is set up by someone who is not UK resident and not at that time concerned with UK tax.

Note that avoiding foreign taxes is OK and won't be caught by the avoidance rules, it's just if the offshore company is set up to avoid UK taxes that it will be caught.

If the individual subsequently comes to the UK he would then have a good claim for the motive exemption. There are also provisions to tax other family members that benefit from the offshore company, but again they would have a good claim for the motive exemption.

If a UK resident owning an interest in an offshore company can take advantage of this, they can use the offshore company as an income shelter avoiding tax on the income. They would obviously need to ensure they didn't extract dividends above their basic rate band otherwise tax would be charged on those.

A good way to access the cash may be to extract tax free after becoming non-resident in the future.

There is no provision for a "clearance" or other advance ruling on the application of the motive defence. Claims to the motive defence may appear in the Foreign Pages of the Tax Return. The additional information section of the return may also be used to provide additional information about a claim.

Note that if you are claiming the motive exemption you still need to declare the income/benefits of the offshore company that are taxed as above. You then enter the exempt amount in box 46.

> **46** If you have omitted income from boxes 11, 13 and 42 because you are claiming an exemption in relation to a transfer of assets, enter the total amount omitted (and give full details in the 'Any other information' box on your tax return)
>
> £ ☐☐☐☐☐☐☐

Recent case on the motive exemption

There was an interesting case on the motive exemption a couple of years ago, which its well worth reviewing.

Facts

The taxpayers' grandfather had built up a very considerable investment in farms and other real property, including an industrial estate. In 1971, certain property was transferred into UK settlements for each of the taxpayers, who had been born in 1962 and 1964 respectively. In the early 1970s the taxpayers immigrated to Jersey with their parents. In 1980, non-resident trustees of all the settlements were appointed in order to avoid paying capital gains tax when the taxpayers reached their eighteenth birthdays.

Jersey companies were also incorporated to take the property to which the taxpayers would become absolutely entitled when they were 18.

Each of the taxpayers (the 'Sons'), on their eighteenth birthday, had signed an assignment of their interest in the industrial estate to Jersey companies.

Their parents were the only two directors of the two companies. Whilst at the time of the transfers, respectively in 1980 and 1982, the two taxpayers were resident with their parents in Jersey, they were resident in the UK in the 1999-2000 and 2000-01 tax years, for which assessments had been made on them under the transfer of asset provisions. The income of each of the two companies in those two years was in the region of £160,000 in each year.

It was accepted by everyone that all of the above conditions for the transfer of asset rules to apply were met. As such the sole determinant as to whether there was a tax liability under the transfer of asset provisions was whether their transfers were protected by the motive defence.

The Sons argued that they could satisfy both of the motive defences as the main purpose of the transfers of the properties to offshore companies was to divorce ownership from management, and put the management responsibility in relation to the properties into the hands of the parents, who were the directors of both companies.

What the Commissioners said

The Commissioners said that there were two motive defences available. One required each taxpayer to demonstrate, that 'the purpose of avoiding liability to taxation was not the purpose or one of the purposes for which the transfer …[was] effected'. The other applied in relation to 'bona fide commercial transactions' and applied if the taxpayers demonstrated that the transfer '… [was] not designed for the purpose of avoiding liability to taxation'. Either one was sufficient to eliminate liability to tax.

The test to be satisfied in relation to bona fide commercial transactions was a less stringent test, referring to the overall design underlying the transaction. In the case of the non-commercial transaction, there was the more onerous test of showing that the purpose of avoiding liability to taxation was not even one of the purposes for which the transaction was effected.

It was clear from the evidence that neither taxpayer had actually any personal purpose in effecting the transactions. However, the transactions were clearly implemented very deliberately, and the purpose or purposes underlying the transactions were those influencing the taxpayers' parents. The purpose for which the taxpayers effected the transactions was simply to do what their parents suggested, and it seemed appropriate to proceed on the basis that they effectively sought to achieve those purposes that influenced their parents.

The Commissioners did not accept that the transactions were designed to separate ownership from management and that that was a bona fide commercial purpose. The grandfather and UK agents were managing the site before and after the transfers, and the transfers had no effect on that. The Sons played virtually no part in the management of the industrial estate until their grandfather relinquished the reins in about 1987.

The Sons had not established that UK tax avoidance was absent from the purposes for which the transfers were made. On the evidence, the commissioners were inclined to think that the ostensible purposes of the transfers were very dubious and not proven, and that on the balance of probabilities the transfers were made largely for purposes connected with the avoidance of UK tax.

So in this case the motive defence did not apply. This shows just how clear the motives need to be. As a matter of law the burden of proof is on you, claiming the motive exemption. In most cases where the exemption is given it's likely that it will fall within one of the two circumstances above.

Note though that although in this case the Sons were non-resident when they made the transfer they were caught by the anti avoidance rules when they subsequently came to live in the UK. The Commissioners still found a motive to avoid UK tax in this case.

It should also be borne in mind that you can still be caught years after making an actual transfer - in this case nearly 20 years later!

Changes in the 2013 Finance Bill

As stated above there is a general motive exemption which prevents liability arising in circumstances where the transactions were not motivated by tax avoidance or were commercial transactions only incidentally motivated by tax avoidance.

However, the exemption is relatively narrow and the European Commission argued that the provisions breach the EU freedoms of establishment and movement of capital.

Therefore HMRC have brought forward proposals to reform the Transfer of asset provisions.

The draft legislation seeks to bring the legislation into compliance with EU law and also to provide clarity in some areas of practical application of the provisions.

Note that these changes take effect from Royal Assent to Finance Bill 2013 but apply with retrospective effect from 6 April 2012.

The main change is a new exemption for freedom of establishment.

New Exemption

A new exemption will apply for situations where the imposition of UK tax liability would constitute an unjustified and disproportionate restriction of the individual's freedom of establishment or movement of capital in EU law.

Under this new exemption, individuals will not be charged to income tax under these rules by reference to a relevant transaction which takes effect after 6 April 2012 where both of the following conditions are met:

- that:

    - the relevant transaction was a genuine transaction;
    - the individual was subject to tax under the transfer of assets rules as a result of that transaction;
    - any such tax charge would contravene EU treaty rights; and

    - the taxpayer can satisfy HMRC that, viewed objectively, the transaction must be considered a genuine transaction

having regard to the arrangements under which it is effected and any other relevant circumstances.

The exemption is restricted to genuine commercial business activities overseas and also transactions which do not involve commercial activities but are nevertheless genuine transactions protected by the single market.

Business transactions will not be regarded as "genuine" unless they are on arm's length terms and give rise to income attributable to economically significant activity that takes place overseas.

"Brass plate" companies would not be regarded as economically significant for this purpose.

Other Changes

- It will be made clearer that double tax agreements do not override these provisions.

- Other changes will clarify the way in which income is matched with benefits received by an individual in circumstances where an individual other than the original transferor is the chargeable person.

- The double charging provisions will be clarified to ensure that the same income is not taxed both under the transfer of assets provisions and also other tax provisions.

- Companies incorporated outside the UK but resident in the UK will no longer be treated as offshore persons for the purposes of this regime.

This was an anomaly of the current provisions.

The new exemption is clearly broader than the existing commercial transactions exemption as it applies even where transactions are motivated by tax avoidance, provided they are genuine.

However it is not yet clear whether the new exemption, restricted to commercial or genuine transactions, will go quite far enough to satisfy the European Commission; the ECJ has previously indicated that only arrangements which are wholly artificial can be counteracted.

Chapter 7

Apportionment Of Capital Gains

As well as income of the offshore company potentially being taxed on UK resident shareholders, if the offshore company realises capital gains when it sells assets, there are separate rules that can tax these gains on UK residents.

How these rules work

These anti-avoidance provisions require the gains of a non-resident 'close' company to be apportioned amongst the member shareholders. Capital gains tax is charged on those who are resident and, in the case of individuals, domiciled in the UK.

The definition of a close company can be complex, however in simple terms it applies to a company that is controlled by its directors or five or fewer shareholders.

The amount apportioned is determined by the shareholders' interest in the company. So in the usual case, it's based on the total shareholdings.

Example

Jack and Jill are the sole shareholders of JackJill Ltd., a company registered in the Cayman Islands. They hold 50% of the shares each and are both UK resident and domiciled. Assuming they allow non-resident directors to run the company and can satisfactorily show that the company is not centrally managed and controlled from the UK, then the attribution of gains legislation would mean that any gains of the offshore company would be attributed to Jack and Jill (50% each). However, if Jack was non-UK domiciled and claiming the remittance basis, the gains would NOT be attributed to him, only to Jill.

Key rules

- This anti avoidance rule isn't subject to a motive defence. So the innocent investor is still caught by these rules and could be subject to CGT on the gains of the offshore company.

- The shareholder can offset personal capital losses against the gains that are apportioned.

- If there is a capital loss in the offshore company, this is also apportioned to the shareholder but it can only be offset against capital gains that are apportioned under these provisions.

- There is a de minimis shareholding limit of 10% before April 2012. This is being increased to 25% by the 2013 Finance Bill for tax years after 5 April 2012. So if a shareholders owns less than 25% of the shares in the offshore company, the capital gains are not apportioned to them.

- Non UK domiciliaries who claim the remittance basis can also be taxed on the foreign gains on the same basis. So providing the offshore company gains are retained overseas there may well be no attribution.

- The 2013 Finance Bill introduced new exemptions

New Exemptions From April 2012

There is already a limited exemption under these CGT anti avoidance rules so that they don't apply to certain gains including those:

- arising on the disposal of an asset used solely for the purposes of a trade carried on by the company wholly outside the UK; or

- arising on the disposal of an asset used, and used only for the purposes of the part carried on outside the UK, of a trade carried on by the company partly within and partly outside the UK; or

- on which the company is chargeable to tax by virtue of trading in the UK through a permanent establishment.

There is also a limited credit for any tax charged under these rules against tax liability on subsequent dividends or liquidation proceeds from the company in the following three years.

At best, therefore, these CGT rules accelerate payment of capital gains tax; at worst it results in additional tax over and above what is payable on the UK resident's actual returns from the investment.

While the section was intended to prevent individuals setting up offshore vehicles to hold assets which they would otherwise have held directly, the section currently has much wider application and potentially applies to any closely held non-UK resident investment company, even if its non-UK investments are commercially driven and not motivated by tax avoidance.

The amendments now proposed are designed to bring the anti avoidance rules into conformity with EU law.

The main changes are as follows:

New Exemption For Overseas Activity

They will introduce a new exemption which excludes gains from "economically significant" activity carried on outside the UK. This will include the provision of goods or services on a commercial basis involving the use of staff, premises, equipment and addition of economic value commensurate with the size and nature of those activities.

New Motive Exemption

There will also be a general motive exemption for gains on disposals where neither the disposal of the asset nor the acquisition or holding of the asset by the non-UK company formed part of a scheme or arrangements to avoid capital gains tax or corporation tax.

This exemption is not restricted to trading companies so should protect investment holding companies set up for reasons other than UK tax avoidance, for example a local company set up to acquire foreign real estate.

Increase In De Minimis Limit

As stated above the participation threshold for attribution of gains will be increased from over 10% to over 25%.

The changes will take effect from Royal Assent to Finance Bill 2013 but with retrospective effect from 6 April 2012.

Inclusion of FHL Activities

The new provisions also expressly include within the current exemption for trades carried on outside the UK, assets which consist of non-UK accommodation or an interest/right in non-UK accommodation where that accommodation has, for certain periods prior to the relevant disposal, been let as furnished holiday accommodation.

Using double tax treaties to avoid the attribution provisions

One of the key issues with a UK resident using an offshore company would be the above anti avoidance provisions that can attribute capital gains to UK shareholders. Using a company established in a suitable treaty jurisdiction can effectively override this.

This is confirmed in the Revenue manuals which state that:

"...You should always check whether there is a double taxation agreement between the UK and the country in which the company making the gain is resident. If there is no double taxation agreement any TCGA92/S13 charge is unaffected. Similarly if the agreement does not refer to capital gains or Capital Gains Tax the charge under TCGA92/S13 is unaffected. But, if the agreement provides that gains of the type realised by the non-resident company are only taxable in that company's country of residence TCGA92/S13 cannot apply..."

HMRC have stated that *"...For example, Article 15(4) of the Kenya/UK Double Taxation Agreement would prevent TCGA92/S13 applying to the disposal of stocks and shares by a company resident in Kenya. Agreements will often treat gains on the disposal of particular types of asset differently..."*

Article 15 (1-4) of the UK-Kenya treaty to which HMRC refers above states:

"...1 Capital gains from the alienation of immovable property, as defined in paragraph (2) of Article 7, may be taxed in the Contracting State in which such property is situated.

2 Capital gains from the alienation of movable property forming part of the business property of a permanent establishment which an enterprise of a Contracting State has in the other Contracting State or of movable property pertaining to a fixed base available to a resident of a Contracting State in the other Contracting State for the purpose of performing professional services, including such gains from the alienation of such a permanent establishment (alone or together with the whole enterprise) or of such a fixed base, may be taxed in the other State.

3 Notwithstanding the provisions of paragraph (2) of this Article, capital gains derived by a resident of a Contracting State from the alienation of ships and aircraft operated in international traffic and movable property pertaining to the operation of such ships and aircraft shall be taxable only in that Contracting State.

4 Capital gains from the alienation of any property other than those mentioned in paragraphs (1), (2) and (3) of this Article shall be taxable only in the Contracting State of which the alienator is a resident..."

Therefore the above effectively states that non real estate and ship/aircraft assets can be taxed in the residence of the company.

Another example is where a Singaporean company is used.

Looking at the Singapore treaty this states:

"...(1) Gains derived by a resident of a Contracting State from the alienation

of immovable property referred to in Article 6 of this Agreement and situated in the other Contracting State may be taxed in that other State.

(2) Gains derived by a resident of a Contracting State from the alienation of:

(a) shares, other than shares traded on a recognised Stock Exchange, deriving at least three-quarters of their value directly or indirectly from immovable property situated in the other Contracting State, or

(b) an interest in a partnership or trust the assets of which derive at least three-quarters of their value directly or indirectly from immovable property situated in the other Contracting State, may be taxed in that other State.

For the purposes of sub-paragraph (b) of this paragraph, assets consisting of shares referred to in sub-paragraph (a) of this paragraph shall be regarded as immovable property.

(3) Gains from the alienation of movable property forming part of the business property of a permanent establishment which an enterprise of a Contracting State has in the other Contracting State or of movable property pertaining to a fixed base available to a resident of a Contracting State in the other Contracting State for the purpose of performing independent personal services, including such gains from the alienation of such a permanent establishment (alone or with the whole enterprise) or of such fixed base, may be taxed in that other State.

(4) Gains derived by a resident of a Contracting State from the alienation of ships or aircraft operated in international traffic by an enterprise of that Contracting State or movable property pertaining to the operation of such ships or aircraft, shall be taxable only in that Contracting State. (5) Gains from the alienation of any property other than that referred to in paragraphs (1),(2), (3) and (4) of this Article shall be taxable only in the Contracting State of which the alienator is a resident..."

Therefore for a Singapore company with UK resident shareholders, providing the gains in the Singapore company are not realised from:

- UK property

- Companies /Partnerships that have at least 75% of their value in UK property
- UK business assets
- Ships/aircraft

The gains would be taxable solely in Singapore and any gains would not be attributed to the UK shareholders.

Looking at the above the main type of asset this will apply to will be shares or other non property investment assets held by the Singapore company.

Of course the other big issue will be ensuring that the management and control are actually carried out overseas, as we've seen in chapter 4.

Chapter 8

Who Can Use An Offshore Company Tax Efficiently?

The previous chapters outline some pretty strict anti avoidance rules that apply to anyone planning to use an offshore company.

So when it's all thrown into the mix who can actually benefit from using offshore companies?

We run through some of the main occasions when offshore companies can be used tax effectively:

Non-UK resident investors

If you're non-UK resident you have a number of tax advantages when it comes to using offshore companies.

Firstly, it would make establishing the central management and control abroad much easier.

Secondly, the UK anti avoidance rules only apply to UK residents or UK ordinarily resident individuals.

So if you are non-resident or if you have foreign family who could run the company and benefit from the company there should be limited UK tax implications.

Even if you're non-resident and are thinking about coming to the UK in the future, the offshore company could be useful. If you're setting it up for foreign, as opposed to UK tax planning reasons, you should have a good claim for the motive defence when you do come back to the UK.

You would still need to ensure that there wasn't a UK trade though, as the profits from this (if carried on via a UK permanent establishment) would still be subject to UK tax.

Non-UK domiciliaries

Non-UK domiciliaries who are claiming the remittance basis, can retain foreign income and capital gains overseas to avoid the anti avoidance rules that attribute income and gains to UK residents.

Non Doms also frequently have foreign family members that can be trusted to assist running offshore companies from overseas.

Non Doms can also hold UK assets via an offshore company to take these assets out of their estate for UK inheritance tax purposes.

We look at the tax planning opportunities available to non doms in the next chapter.

Individuals looking ahead and are interested in avoiding CGT.

If the plan was to be non-resident in the future an offshore company could be used in the knowledge that at the date of the disposal no gain would be attributed to them. Alternatively they could sell shares in the company free of CGT anyway as a non UK resident.

Multiple Ownership

For CGT purposes only, the anti avoidance rules only attribute the capital gains to someone who holds more than 25% of the shares.

So you could hold UK or foreign investment assets via an offshore company, and the capital gains on disposals could be free of CGT.

Avoiding Benefitting From The Company

The income tax anti avoidance rules only apply where you have made a transfer to the company and you or your spouse has the power to enjoy the income of the offshore company.

Therefore it could be thought that so long as you avoid having any right to benefit from the offshore company income you could avoid these provisions.

It's not quite this simple however, as an individual is defined as having power to enjoy in a number of key situations.

One of the key problems if you remain a shareholder would be the second situation which applies where the income increases the value to you of assets held by you or for your benefit. It catches the classic operation at which these provisions were aimed i.e. the sale of income producing assets to an offshore company in exchange for shares or debentures.

Therefore if an individual was a UK resident shareholder there would be a power to enjoy and the provisions would apply unless he could claim the motive exemption which would be declared on the tax return).

Sound Commercial Reason

The motive defence is always relevant for income tax purposes. So anyone looking at using an offshore company as an income tax shelter and who has a sound commercial reason for the use of the company could use the offshore company without UK tax being charged on the foreign trading profits.

Overseas Subsidiaries

As we'll see in a later chapter, offshore companies that are established as subsidiaries of UK companies are subject to separate anti avoidance rules.

In many cases the new changes that are applying from 2012 will mean that providing the offshore company has profits of less than £500,000, these rules won't apply to them. This will mean that profits can be retained in the offshore company free of UK taxes.

Chapter 9

Using An Offshore Holding Company For Non Doms

Non Doms, along with non-UK residents are potentially in the best position in terms of UK tax to make use of offshore companies and trusts. As we've seen the key problems with using an offshore company are:

- the problems over establishing management and control overseas
- the anti avoidance rules that can attribute both income and capital gains to UK residents

Both of these still apply to non doms, although there are specific exemptions from the latter.

Ignoring these issues though what are the benefits of an offshore company for non doms?

One of the benefits could be in terms of an offshore holding company. Assume you have the following scenario:

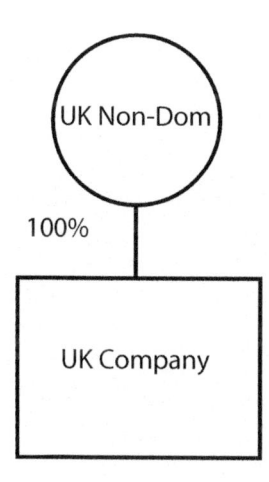

```
        ( UK Non-Dom )
             |
           100%
             |
        [ UK Company ]
```

The UK resident non-UK domiciliary owns all the shares in a UK trading company. The profits of the trade would be subject to corporation tax at rates up to 23% (from April 2013). Any profits extracted from the company would be subject to UK income tax, irrespective of the shareholders' non dom status as the dividends have a UK source.

What if the non dom changes the structure to:

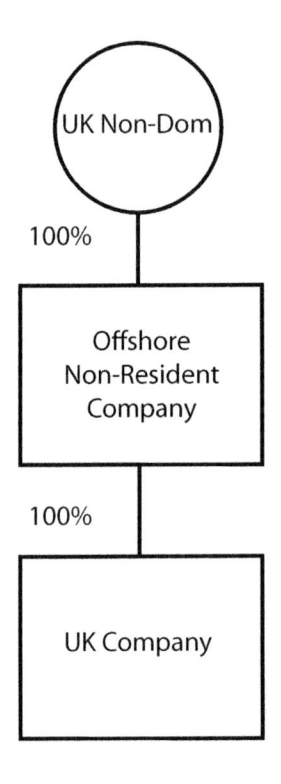

```
        ┌─────────────┐
        │ UK Non-Dom  │
        └─────────────┘
              │
            100%
              │
      ┌───────────────┐
      │   Offshore    │
      │ Non-Resident  │
      │   Company     │
      └───────────────┘
              │
            100%
              │
      ┌───────────────┐
      │  UK Company   │
      └───────────────┘
```

In this case the UK trading company is owned by an offshore, non-UK resident company, which is in turn owned by the UK resident non dom.

In this case the UK trading company is still subject to corporation tax on its trading profits, but dividends are paid potentially free of tax to the non-resident holding company. Dividends then paid from the non-resident company could potentially be retained abroad free of income tax.

By interposing an offshore company, it provides for dividends to be paid out free of UK income tax.

There are as you'd expect a number of obstacles to achieving this:

Firstly the company needs to be classed as non-resident, otherwise dividends would have a UK source. As such the company would need to be managed and controlled from overseas. If control is actually exercised by the non dom shareholder in the UK clearly this would not be met.

Secondly the non dom would need to claim the remittance basis. This means they would usually lose the benefit of the personal allowance and annual CGT exemption and if they've been UK resident for more than 7 years would also need to pay the £30,000 tax charge (rising to £50,000 for more than 12 years of UK residence after April 2012).

Thirdly they'd need to consider the anti avoidance provisions. If they're claiming the remittance basis they can avoid these by retaining the income in the company overseas. If not, there's a risk that the offshore company income would be taxed on the UK non dom. If they could argue for a motive defence or exclude themselves from benefiting from the company they could potentially avoid this.

Using an offshore holding company could be a useful mechanism for non doms to utilise UK trading profits overseas free of UK tax. They could also gift or transfer cash to 'non-relevant persons' (e.g. adult children) for them to bring back to the UK for their own benefit without this being classed as a remittance.

IHT Advantages For Non Doms

Non UK domicilaries are only subject to UK inheritance tax ('IHT') on their UK estate. They therefore have a significant IHT benefit from using an offshore company to UK assets. By holding UK assets via an offshore company they effectively swap the UK assets for overseas assets (i.e. the shares in the offshore company). The foreign shares which would reflect the value of the underlying assets held in the company, would then be exempt from UK inheritance tax.

For this reason many non doms favour an offshore holding structure to purchase UK investment property.

Where the purchase is of UK residential property an offshore company is likely to be most attractive where the property value is less than £2,000,000 or it is planned to let the property on arm's length terms.

If a UK residential property was held by an offshore company with a UK shareholder and the property was retained for the shareholder (or their family's) occupation there are a number of additional anti avoidance rules that could apply (including a CGT charge on disposal and an annual tax charge based on the value of the property).

Chapter 10

Overseas Trading

Using a new offshore subsidiary or a branch

If you want to do business in another country two of the options you have are:

- Incorporate a new company offshore and use this to carry out the overseas business, or

- Establish a branch of the existing UK company and carry out the trade via the branch.

Note that in physical terms the two would look more or less identical from overseas: there could be overseas premises, staff and equipment.

The main difference would be in the ownership. If the overseas trade was owned by the UK company it would be a branch, if owned by an offshore company it could be a subsidiary.

Deciding whether to use a branch or subsidiary will have significant implications on how the profits from the overseas trade will be taxed.

In particular the tax treatment of foreign branches has changed after 19 July 2011.

Old treatment

Prior to 19 July 2011, the main difference between the two is that the profits of a branch will be classed as part of the UK company's taxable profits along with its UK trading profits.

The branch profits will usually be separated from the UK trading income if the branch is actually controlled from overseas, and therefore it could be taxed as income from an overseas 'possession' as opposed to trading income. This difference though is not all that important, and the key point is that the full profits of the overseas branch will be subject to UK corporation tax.

By contrast, if an overseas subsidiary is used, and provided the company is non-UK resident (in other words, the overseas directors exercise control), the profits of the overseas subsidiary should not be subject to UK corporation tax.

As we've seen earlier, the company will be a non-UK resident provided it's not incorporated in the UK, and its central management and control is overseas. In addition, provided the overseas company does not fall within the controlled foreign company provisions (see below) the only time that the UK company will be subject to corporation tax is when the overseas company declares a dividend.

This would therefore give the UK company an element of control over when it incurs a UK tax charge (for example, during an accounting period of otherwise low income).

Another key difference is that if a branch is used and it sustains a loss, this can often be offset against other UK trading profits.

However, if you use an overseas subsidiary and that incurs a loss, the opportunities for it to utilise its loss will be restricted. It could only be used against UK profits where the overseas company is not able to offset the loss against any overseas profits.

An overseas branch could claim tax relief under the capital allowances legislation for assets used in the trade when calculating the taxable profits in the UK company. If you used a subsidiary no capital allowances would be due (unless the overseas country has its own capital allowance rules).

Finally, if you use a subsidiary, this will be classed as another 'associated company' which would reduce the tax bands for calculating the UK company's corporation tax. For example, this could have the effect that the UK company would pay 23% corporation tax on profits exceeding £750,000, as opposed to £1.5 million.

The fact that losses are given more flexible relief in a branch means that, where an overseas operation is expected to incur losses in the first few years of trading, it is often advisable to initially trade overseas using a branch (with full relief for losses in the UK) and then transfer the trade to an overseas subsidiary when it is about to become profitable (to eliminate UK tax on the profits).

New Rules

As from 19 July 2011 there has been a significant change to the tax treatment of foreign branches of UK companies.

If an (irrevocable) election is made, all profits and losses can remain permanently outside the scope of UK corporation tax.

There are certain conditions to be met, but if an election is made the key points are:

- The election has to apply to all foreign branches, not just selected ones.

- Capital and income profits and losses are covered.

- Assets utilised in the overseas branch are, for tax purposes, transferred to it from the UK company at a no gain no loss value at the outset of the election taking effect.

Inevitably there are detailed anti-avoidance provisions to prevent abuse.

Certain types of businesses are excluded from the new rules, including:

- Long term insurance businesses, being primarily life assurance and permanent health insurance;

- Companies which derive their income mainly from making investments;

- Certain international air transport and shipping companies; and

- The profits of close companies which stem from chargeable gains.

Additionally, smaller companies can only make the new election if their foreign branches are situated in territories that have a double taxation treaty with the UK, that includes a non-discrimination clause.

A small company is, broadly, one with no more than 50 staff and with either annual turnover or a balance sheet total of less than €10 million.

So if you have a small company and are setting up a branch in a country which the UK has a treaty with you would need to weigh up making the election as it is irrevocable, not just for that branch but for all future branches.

Losses wouldn't be allowable for offset against UK profits, but on the other side branch profits wouldn't be taxed.

If however, the foreign jurisdiction levied tax on the profits that would fully cover any UK liability under the double tax relief provisions, it may be preferable not to make the election. This would then ensure that losses were still available.

Transferring a trade to an offshore company & UK tax

If you carry out a trade via a UK company this will automatically be UK resident and as such subject to corporation tax on its worldwide income and gains.

You can't 'migrate' the company to transfer it overseas. The only way you could achieve this result would be by establishing treaty residence overseas.

This involves establishing the effective management and control under a double tax treaty as overseas.

Another option though would be to simply transfer the trade from the UK to an offshore company. The UK company would then be a shell company and simply wound up. You could also retain cash in the company if you wished and extract this as a capital distribution on the winding up. It would then be subject to CGT at 10% or 28% depending on if full Entrepreneurs Relief was due or not.

What are the tax implications of a transfer of a trade to an offshore company?

Transferring your trade to an offshore company will have two main tax implications:

Firstly the transfer of the trade from the UK company to the offshore company would be a disposal for capital gains purposes. This isn't a specific rule that applies to transfers to offshore companies but rather is a general rule that applies on the transfer of any assets out of a company.

Therefore irrespective of the disposal consideration that is actually transferred from the offshore company to the UK any capital gain in the UK company would be based on the market value of the assets transferred. You would therefore need to value the assets that were transferred to the offshore company. This would include plant/machinery, any land or property but usually goodwill is the largest asset transferred.

Secondly the other key tax issue on the transfer of the trade overseas is that the transfer would also be treated as a distribution (i.e. a dividend) to the shareholders given that they have extracted value from the company.

The amount of the distribution would be the undervalue at which the trade was transferred. Note though that non UK residents are only charged to UK income tax on dividends to the extent that tax was deducted at source. Given that there would be no tax deducted at source it may be possible to avoid income tax on the distribution. The alternative would be for the offshore company to pay the full market value to the UK company for the trade. There would then be no distribution on the transfer but the shareholders could extract the cash as non-residents free of further income tax.

It's also worth noting that there would be no relief for losses unless there was a UK trade carried on.

UK trade?

The other issue is that even if you did use an offshore non-UK resident company, the UK would still tax profits that arise from a UK trade carried out via a UK permanent establishment. Therefore you would need to be very careful to ensure that there was no UK trade/permanent establishment. We look at this in a separate chapter.

You should in any case think very carefully before making a transfer and should take detailed advice. As stated above, a capital gain would arise in the UK company on the assets transferred - including goodwill.

This gain in the UK company would effectively be the same as the deemed tax charge on a non-UK company when it migrates overseas (i.e. the uplift in value to market value is subject to corporation tax).

Mechanics of a transfer

If you did want to go ahead with the transfer you should draw up a disposal agreement for the transfer of the trade & assets listing the assets transferred. There is no requirement for there to be financial consideration for the transfer. You would also need to arrange for a board resolution approving the transfer from the UK company.

After the transfer

After you've transferred the trade you'll be left with a shell UK company. This could be wound up/struck off relatively simply. If the company held cash assets you could extract these as a capital distribution. If you were non-resident CGT could be avoided. If not you'd be taxed at 10% or 28% depending on whether Entrepreneurs Relief is due or not.

The tax position of the offshore company & the trade would then depend on general principles i.e. whether the company is clearly established as controlled overseas and whether there is a UK trade.

Chapter 11

Controlled Foreign Companies

One of the advantages in using an overseas subsidiary company is that the UK parent company would not be charged tax on the profits of the overseas non-UK resident subsidiary... provided the UK CFC rules don't apply.

The CFC rules would therefore be of great importance to any company that was looking to establish an overseas subsidiary.

If the CFC rules apply they will ensure that part of the overseas company's profits are taxed in the hands of UK companies who hold an interest in the CFC.

You should note that the UK CFC regime will not apply if you are an individual owning an overseas company.

Before falling within the CFC rules a company would firstly need to meet the definition of a 'controlled foreign company'.

A CFC is defined as:

- A non-UK resident company, and
- A company controlled from the UK, and
- A company subject to overseas tax which is less than 75% of the equivalent UK tax.

Therefore the CFC provisions are going to apply to overseas companies established in low tax countries. What you'd need to do is to calculate the company's profits and find out what the overseas tax charge is.

You'd then calculate the UK tax liability and if the overseas tax paid is less than three-quarters of the UK tax, the overseas company could fall within the CFC provisions.

Before getting into the nitty-gritty of the new regime applying from 2012 it's worthwhile noting that the big news for SMEs is that the de-minimis profits limit has been raised from £50,000 per annum to £500,000 per annum, an increase of tenfold. Most SMEs will therefore fall outside of the CFC rules.

How the new CFC rules will apply from 2012

New rules for controlled foreign companies (CFCs) have been introduced in the 2012 Finance Bill. These include significant changes in the CFC regime to better reflect the globalised economy in which businesses operate.

Why have a CFC regime?

A CFC regime is needed to protect the artificial diversion of profits to low tax jurisdictions. In particular, rules are needed to deal with monetary assets and intellectual property which offer the greatest scope for profit diversion.

In the 2011 Budget it was announced that the new CFC regime would include a finance company partial exemption. Consideration is also being given as to whether there are limited circumstances in which a full exemption may be appropriate for finance companies. The aim is to provide businesses based in the UK with the flexibility to invest capital to meet commercial needs throughout the world and to allow future profits earned on that capital to be repatriated to the UK without a UK tax charge.

Aims Of The New CFC Regime

The aims of the new CFC regime, as stated in the latest consultation document, are to:

- target and impose a CFC charge on artificially diverted profits so that UK profits are fairly taxed;

- exempt foreign profits where there is no artificial diversion of UK profits; and

- not tax profits arising from genuine economic activities undertaken offshore.

Overview of new regime

The new regime is targeted at situations that pose the highest risk of artificial diversion of UK profits. The rules will apply to individual entities. A proportionate approach is adopted such that where a CFC charge applies it will only apply to those profits which have been diverted artificially from the UK. Genuine foreign profits are exempt from the charge.

The regime also seeks to recognise that most CFCs are held for genuine commercial reasons and do not pose a risk to the UK tax base. Consequently a number of exemptions will apply, including a general purpose exemption providing companies with the opportunity to demonstrate that they have not artificially diverted profits from the UK.

The new regime will in many ways operate in a similar way to the existing regime. It will identify lowly taxed foreign companies controlled from the UK.

The existence of a number of exemptions will remove from the CFC regime those CFCs that do not artificially divert profits away from the UK. The exemptions, however, are being modernised.

To provide a more territorial approach to the taxation of branches, Finance Act 2011 introduced an opt-in exemption for foreign branches. Equivalent protection is proposed for foreign subsidiaries and exempt foreign branches.

The new regime is essentially a risk-based regime that focuses on CFCs where there is a high risk that they are being used to artificially divert profits away from the UK.

Three-step approach

The new regime will follow a three-step approach:

(1) identifying CFCs;

(2) exempting CFCs that pose a low risk to the UK tax base;

(3) calculating a CFC charge when profits have been artificially diverted from the UK.

The first step is to identify a CFC. For the purposes of the new regime a CFC is a company that is under UK control, is resident outside the UK and has profits that are taxed at a lower effective rate than if the company were resident in the UK (by applying the lower level of tax test).

The CFC regime recognises that most CFCs undertake genuine commercial activity that does not artificially divert profits away from the UK. Therefore the regime features a number of exemptions to exclude those CFCs.

Having identified a CFC, the second step is to see whether one or more of the exemptions are in point. The exemptions are as follows:

The first test to check is probably the excluded territories exemption. HMT will publish a list of those jurisdictions where they are happy that the local corporation tax will be no less than 75% of the UK equivalent liability. Any companies resident in these jurisdictions will not be CFCs.

As stated above there is a low profits exemption which means that if the overseas company profits are less than £500,000 it won't be a CFC.

Next there is the low profit margin test. Essentially the CFC must have a very low profit margin of less than 10% of cost. Cost cannot include any related party expenditure.

Next we move onto the business trading income safe harbour. Here the CFC needs to meet a variety of tests.

These include having a business premises available locally, incurring no more than 20% of overall expenditure on supplies from UK sources, invoicing no more than 20% of total turnover to UK customers, there being a limited connection to UK orientated intellectual property rights, and the management cost of the CFC being at least 80% incurred outside the UK. This safe harbour approach is helpful, but currently the rules are conceptual and there is little in the way of guidance or examples. The area of IP is one of the great uncertainties of the CFC legislation as the way in which 'connection' is determined is still largely up for debate.

There is an exemption for CFCs that only let property in the foreign jurisdiction. There are also exemptions for incidental non-trading finance income.

There is a new exemption for finance companies set up in low tax jurisdictions which meet a number of criteria. This reduces the rate of UK corporation tax that might be levied down to just 5.5%. It is unlikely that there will be too many SMEs affected by this specific provision and others related to it including the captive insurance business rules.

Overarching the CFC rules is a 'gateway test'. This test will allow taxpayers and advisers to very quickly rule a company out of the CFC regime where it meets a number of criteria.

You can see more on using an offshore subsidiary tax efficiently in our guide:

<u>Offshore Tax Planning For UK Companies</u>

Chapter 12

EU VAT Planning With An Offshore Structure

Anyone trading from within Europe will usually be interested in opportunities to reduce both tax and VAT burdens. There are lots of options and opportunities available, but using a Swiss trading company to reduce VAT can be highly attractive for certain traders, particularly where this is combined with a tax efficient offshore structure.

Who it applies to:

The typical company that can reap the benefits will be a company carrying out business to consumer (B2C) transactions for VAT purposes. Usually in this case VAT is charged at the place of supply which, in the context of the "supply of services to a person who is not a relevant business person" is defined as "where the supplier belongs".

There are specific provisions for anyone trading online that can (in simple terms) mean that VAT is charged where the customer is based. These would need to be considered. However, one of the key exceptions would be where you are providing services to customers on an individual, personalised basis. The activities would then not be deemed as falling within the provisions of the EU 'E-Business' Directive and VAT would be based on where the supplying company is.

Opportunity

In this case it is possible to create a company in Switzerland. This is outside the EU but which is part of EFTA and so largely complies with European VAT legislation, (as defined under the Sixth VAT Directive 2006/112/EC). The Swiss company will sell to EU (including the UK) customers with VAT charged at 8% as opposed to the current 20%. This would dramatically increase the profitability of most companies.

The current VAT regulations re EU B2C place of supply will stay in force until 2015 at the very earliest -- but there is currently no reason to believe that this situation will change even in 2015. Given that such a change would need not only the appropriate approval at the European Commission level but also an appropriate preliminary phase before implementation, it can be stated with some confidence that the current EU VAT B2C regulations will remain in force for many years to come.

In terms of corporation tax the effective rate of Corporate Tax in Switzerland ranges from 14.5% to 33.5%, the average being 21.6% which is more or less on a par with the UK. However an offshore structure could be set up to significantly reduce the Swiss profits.

Offshore Structure

There are lots of different variations on this but for example the Swiss shareholder could control a Panama or Seychelles Private Interest Foundation which in turn would own a Cypriot company.

The Cypriot company would have an inter-company agreement with the Swiss company to invoice it for services provided, leaving the Swiss company with substantially reduced profits (this would need to be at a sufficient level to satisfy the Swiss tax authorities).

This would then ensure that the the vast majority of profits ended up in Cyprus with its 10% Corporate Tax rate.

This structure could be added to in terms of privacy with the Shareholder owning an SPV in Delaware so that his/her name doesn't appear on the charter documents of the Seychelles/Panama Foundation which it owns.

You could also expand the structure further by having the Foundation holding shares in a BVI holding company (inserted to facilitate the later selling a share of the business) which owns a Cypriot company (trading to the USA) which in turn owns both a Swiss company (trading to the UK/EU and paying the Cypriot parent company for management expertise) and a new UK limited company (which provides administrative support to the Swiss company).

The individual could then extract funds as a freelance management consultant of the Cypriot company, leaving the remainder of the profits to accumulate in the Foundation for subsequent investment in property via a Cypriot company.

UK Issues

Key UK tax issues would be establishing the central management and control was overseas and avoiding the UK anti avoidance rules.

Therefore this type of structure should ideally be used by a non-UK resident individual looking to trade in the EU/Internationally.

Providing there was then no UK permanent establishment there would be no UK tax on the profits generated.

If a UK company was used as a recharge company this would of course be taxed in the UK on these profits.

Chapter 13

Trading In The UK With An Offshore Company

It's a common fallacy that simply establishing an offshore company is a simple method to avoid paying UK taxes. This is not always the case and you need to ensure you pay careful attention to the UK tax legislation given much will depend on the type of income being earned and your own residence position.

In particular, the old chestnut of using a non-resident company to trade in the UK is one of the most complex areas. However it may well be the case that in this situation an offshore company could be the best option. To keep it simple, lets assume you yourself are a non-resident and you're interested in doing business with the UK.

You could of course use a UK company to carry out your trade. If you did, you'd be subject to UK corporation tax on the company's profits. For many non-residents, using an offshore, non-resident company is preferable.

A non-resident company would only be subject to UK taxes if the central management and control of the company was carried out in the UK. If you are the director/shareholder and are non-UK resident, it would be rare that the company would be controlled from the UK

So on this basis, if you are non-UK resident you should have few problems establishing the company as non-UK resident. As we've seen this would mean that the company would not be charged to UK corporation tax on it's overseas income.

If the non-resident company's activities in the UK do not amount to trading there is no charge to UK corporation tax on the profits arising, even if the cash is derived from the UK. However, there is a distinction between trading in the UK and trading with the UK. Trading by non-residents with the UK, as opposed to in the UK, does not bring the non-resident within the UK domestic charging provisions.

When looking at an offshore company, the UK doesn't just look to see if there is a UK trade. It will first look to see if there is a UK permanent establishment (they used to look at whether there was a branch or agency). If a non-resident company trades in the UK through a permanent establishment/branch or agency the tax legislation says that its chargeable profits shall include `any trading income arising directly or indirectly through or from the permanent establishment/branch or agency'.

Therefore you'd need to first assess whether a UK permanent establishment/branch or agency arose.

According to the Corporation Tax Acts `branch or agency' means any factorship, agency, receivership, branch or management.

This is very important as if there is no UK permanent establishment there may well be no UK tax charge.

A foreign company can be classed as having a permanent establishment in the UK if:

- it has a fixed place of business in the UK
- it has a UK dependent agent

The concept of an agency is important and it is also a difficult and specialised element of UK law and should be looked at in detail. However briefly an agent represents a person (known as the 'principal') in accordance with the terms of the agreement to act. That agreement may be oral or in writing and it is called the agent's authority. In representing the principal the agent may bring about a legal relationship between that principal and a third party.

For instance if any UK salespeople do not have the power to bind the offshore company (i.e. the power to conclude a contract) this would signify there was no agency.

We look at the scope of the agency provisions shortly. However aside from these, when looking at any offshore companies UK taxable presence the UK taxman would first look to identify if you have a permanent establishment that trades in the UK, e.g. an office, and secondly, if not whether there is simply a trade in the UK.

Actually what constitutes trading in the UK can be difficult to determine. However a key consideration will be where contracts are signed and where the main revenue generating services are carried out.

Providing contracts are signed overseas, the actual income producing business activities are overseas and there is no branch of the new venture in the UK, it should not be charged to UK corporation tax.

UK Permanent Establishment

This requires all these essential features to be present:

a. there must be a geographic place of business

b. the place of business must be fixed, that is, have a certain degree of permanence, and

c. the non-resident's business must be carried on through this fixed place of business.

This makes it clear that there is a geographical condition within the fixed place of business definition. There must be a distinct place of business being used for carrying on the business.

Therefore, for instance, a travelling salesmen selling products from door to door would not have a fixed place of business in the UK.

So one case where there will not be a permanent establishment is where there is no fixed place of business in the UK. If for instance you're selling products via a website to UK customers it's unlikely this would be a fixed place of business and there should be no UK tax charge.

The other option to avoid the permanent establishment provisions is where there is a fixed place of business but this is specifically excluded from being a permanent establishment.

There is no permanent establishment in the UK if the activities here in relation to the business as a whole, are preparatory or auxiliary in character. The statutory definition gives some examples of activities that are preparatory or auxiliary as follows:

a. The use of facilities for the purpose of storage, display or delivery of goods or merchandise belonging to the company,

b. The maintenance of a stock of goods or merchandise belonging to the company for the purpose of storage, display or delivery,

c. The maintenance of a stock of goods or merchandise belonging to the company for the purpose of processing by another person,

d. Purchasing goods or merchandising, or collecting information, for the company.

Therefore for example if you used a UK warehouse to purchase and hold stock with the key revenue generating activities being undertaken offshore there should also be no UK permanent establishment.

Using an offshore company

The best option if you're non-resident may be to use a non-UK resident company. This would completely avoid UK corporation tax and also reduce any UK disclosure.

You could consider a company in the Isle of Man which offers 0% corporation tax and can also obtain an EU VAT number.

If you're non-resident there should be no issues in terms of the company being UK resident and if there is no UK permanent establishment there would be no UK corporation tax on the profits. In addition if the receipts are not royalties they wouldn't be subject to UK withholding tax. Receipts could be payable into either a UK or IOM bank account and based on the assumptions above there should be no UK tax due.

Double tax treaties would not be an issue with an offshore company as there is unlikely to be a treaty in place. Note that there is a limited treaty between the UK and IOM which effectively provides that profits in the UK would be taxable to the extent there is a permanent establishment. This is therefore similar to the UK's s domestic provisions.

If using an offshore company was not an option and you wanted to use a UK entity, you could use either a UK company or a UK limited liability partnership.

UK company

If using a UK company, it would be charged to UK corporation tax on its worldwide income and gains.

The most effective option would be to use the UK company as an agency company contracting with the clients but not being classed as an agent for the definition of the permanent establishment provisions (e.g. no power to bind the offshore principal/independent agent and no UK fixed place of business).

The receipts would be taken via the UK company, and paid to you or another offshore entity less a small commission (e.g. 5%). The commission rate would need to be set at a market rate and the income of the company would be the 5% received. It could then offset any expenses etc. before corporation tax was applied.

The UK company would not be taxed on the entire income it received on behalf of an offshore principal but it would clearly be taxed on its commission receipts.

The downsides to this are that UK accounts and an annual return would need to be filed along with corporation tax returns. Shareholders and Directors details would need to be disclosed to the UK tax authorities.

UK reporting

In terms of the accounts for the UK company it would be essential to determine whether for accounting purposes it acted as principal or agent.

UK reporting standards state that in order for a company to be viewed as a principal it should normally have exposure to all significant benefits and risks associated with at least one of the following:

(a) Selling price: the ability, within economic constraints, to establish the selling price with the customer, either directly or, where the selling price of an item is fixed, indirectly by providing additional goods or services or adjusting the terms of a linked transaction; or

(b) Stock: exposure to the risks of damage, slow movement and obsolescence, and changes in suppliers' prices.

Where the seller has not disclosed that it is acting as agent, there is a rebuttable presumption that it is acting as principal.

Additional factors which indicate that a seller may be acting as principal include:

(a) performance of part of the services, or modification to the goods supplied;

(b) assumption of credit risk; and

(c) discretion in supplier selection.

By contrast where a seller acts as agent it will not normally be exposed to the majority of the benefits and risks associated with the transaction. Agency arrangements will typically include the following characteristics:

(a) the seller has disclosed the fact that it is acting as agent;

(b) once the seller has confirmed its customer's order with a third party, the seller will normally have no further involvement in the performance of the ultimate supplier's contractual obligations;

(c) the amount that the seller earns is predetermined, being either a fixed fee per transaction or a stated percentage of the amount billed to the customer; and

(d) the seller bears no stock or credit risk, other than in circumstances where it receives additional consideration from the ultimate supplier in return for its assumption of this risk.

Where the substance of a transaction is that the company acts as agent, it should report as turnover in the accounts the commission received in return for its performance under the agency arrangement.

Any amounts received that are payable to the offshore principal would not be included in the agent's turnover.

You'd therefore need to determine whether the UK company could be classed as an agent for the purposes of the accounts.

As stated above it looks at the substance of the transaction and there is a rebuttable presumption that if there's no disclosure of the principal that the UK company would be the principal (and therefore report all the turnover and the subsequent payments back to the offshore company).

Limited Liability Partnership ('LLP')

The alternative option would be to use an LLP. This is a pass-through entity for UK tax purposes and therefore the income would be attributed to you personally. Providing the profits are not profits of a UK trade and you are non-UK resident there would be no UK income tax charge on the profits.

This therefore has an advantage over the UK Ltd. company above in that it can avoid all UK tax.

In terms of disclosure the notes to the Partnership return specifically state that '…Where all the partners are not resident in the UK, the Partnership

Tax Return should enter only the profits arising from UK operations...'. Therefore if the partnership had no UK trading profit the partnership return would effectively be blank.

The downside of an LLP is that it would need to file accounts with companies house showing it's profit and loss account and balance sheet, even though it may conduct its business entirely overseas.

Double Tax Treaties

If you are resident in a country with which the UK has a double taxation treaty then the UK will consider the provisions of the treaty as well as domestic law before they decide whether there is a liability to UK tax. A treaty may exempt where the domestic law would charge and a treaty may provide for a liability which the UK does not enforce.

The standard OECD model treaty essentially asks

- does the non-resident, being a resident of country A, carry on its business through a permanent establishment in country B the treaty partner?

The standard treaty will cover this in Article 5 of the treaty.

The approach of Article 5 is essentially that which many European countries adopt in their domestic law. These countries are interested in foreigners who have income arising in their countries or whose trading is concerned in a very intimate way with their countries. It is usual to find in their domestic law that they define a whole range of income arising in their country. Such income is taxable when belonging to non-residents. As far as trading is concerned, the main question such countries will ask is - does this foreigner carry on business in our country through a permanent establishment.

Article 5 of the OECD Model is based on that idea and goes into some detail asking whether there is a branch, an office, factory or workshop or the like fixed place of business through which the business of the non-resident is wholly or partly carried on. 'Carrying on business' is a far wider concept than our domestic idea of 'trading in'.

All sorts of activity might be included in the former expression which are not within the latter. And because it is so wide there need to be exceptions to let out activities which, although they constitute the carrying on of business, are not the sort of activities a country would wish to tax. Such activities are listed in Article 5(4) and include things like storage, display and delivery of goods and activities which are of a preparatory or ancillary nature - all of them things which in our domestic law would not amount to trading in the UK.

Therefore of crucial importance in this area is any double tax treaty and this should be reviewed. However, provided the non UK resident company does not have UK permanent establishment there should be no charge to UK corporation or income tax under either the UK's domestic rules or any relevant tax treaties. Simply providing services from overseas, with no significant UK role in the provision of the service should therefore not be caught by these provisions.

So there you have it, when providing goods or services to the UK, you need to ensure that you use an offshore entity and that:

- it does not amount to a UK trade
- there is no UK permanent establishment in accordance with the terms of any double taxation treaty.

Provided all these are satisfied you can conduct activities in the UK without being caught within the UK tax net.

Tax treatment of UK agents

As we've seen above an offshore company can have a permanent establishment if either:

- It has a fixed place of business in the UK, or
- It has a UK dependent agent

This means that offshore companies that don't themselves operate a UK 'base' to carry out UK activities won't be subject to UK corporation tax on the UK trading profits unless they have a UK dependent agent.

Therefore as well as looking at whether there is a geographical/fixed place of business in the UK, it's also essential to consider whether there is a UK agent.

What is an agent?

An agent is anybody (be it an individual, partnership or company) that represents another party (known as the principal) in accordance with the terms of an agreement in place between them.

The key point is that an agent can bring about a legal relationship between the principal and a third party. As above it's common where a UK agent makes a contract with UK customers to sell some goods on behalf of a foreign principal.

You could have a situation where:

A German company wants to sell widgets to car dealers in the UK. Instead of dealing with them directly they could use a UK company to act on their behalf.

The UK company would source customers, deal with customer service issues, take payment in exchange for an agency fee. This fee is usually based on a % of the business it generates. The key point though is that the accounts of the UK company would not show the proceeds from the sale of the widgets as earnings of the UK company.

The UK company would just be taxed on any agency fee it receives, less the associated expenses that it incurs.

So whilst the UK company is taxed only on the agency fee, the big earnings (from the sale of the widgets) may well accumulate offshore. In this case the UK taxman would want to see whether there is a UK permanent establishment to try and tax the widget earnings. There is no fixed place of business in the UK, so the taxman would look to see if the UK agent could be classed as a permanent establishment.

The tax legislation states that the following type of agency is a permanent establishment for UK tax purposes:

'...an agent acting on behalf of the company where the agent has and habitually exercises their authority to do business on behalf of the company. As long as that agent is not of independent status acting in the ordinary course of his business...'

So this is pretty clear then and if you have an agency arrangement in the UK you'll need to consider whether this could be caught by this provision. In practice this is very important as it could well make the difference between the earnings be taxed in the UK or not.

Dependent agent v independent agent

One of the key issues from the above is that the tax legislation makes a distinction between dependent agents and independent agents.

If you're looking to gain the tax exemption you'll need to show that the agency was an independent agency.

Whether an agent is an independent agent will depend on the nature of the relationship between the non-resident and the agent. If the relationship between them is the same as a relationship between independent businesses dealing with each other at arm's length then the agent will be 'an independent agent'.

A good example is an agent that acted for a few independent and unconnected businesses. If they acted on the same terms with these and an offshore principal it would be difficult for the Revenue to argue that the agent had not been acting in the ordinary course of his business.

Planning for an agency arrangement

The type of issues that the Revenue will look at when considering whether there is a dependent or independent agency arrangement are:

- the number of unrelated principals that the agent acted for;
- the extent of the business activities customarily carried out by independent agents in the particular business area;

- the extent of the obligations that the agent has to the non-resident;

- whether the agent is subject to comprehensive control;

- whether the agent bears the entrepreneurial risk for the business that the agent carries out;

- the degree of reliance on the agent's special skill and knowledge by the principal in the business.

Clearly if you use a genuinely independent, third party agency company to act on the behalf of the offshore company there would be a reduced risk of an argument that the agent was a dependent agent, given it would probably act for other principals as well.

If this was not an option and you were to use an associated company to act as an agent you would need to structure the agency arrangement more carefully. Even if the agent was a subsidiary company this would not in itself mean that it could not be an independent agent. You would though need to ensure that the arrangements were conducted on an arm's length basis.

There would need to be an agency agreement that specified the rights and duties of the parties including the agency fee. In many cases the agency fee would be based on a percentage of the business that the agent generates. In any case, it should be ensured that there is evidence to support the arm's length nature of the agency arrangements.

Agency and double tax treaties

As well as the UK domestic law, there are also the terms of any double tax treaties to consider. These would override the UK domestic legislation, and given the fact that the UK has so many treaties these are vital.

The treaties adopt a similar rule to the UK domestic law, in that they state that an agent can constitute a permanent establishment. The Model treaty that many of the UK treaties follow deems an agent to be a permanent establishment if the agent has and habitually exercises an authority to conclude contracts in the name of the enterprise of the treaty partner state, unless the agent is an agent of independent status.

Therefore again you would need to consider whether the agent can be classed as an independent agent.

The model treaty also excludes brokers, general commission agents and any other agents of independent status from being treated as permanent establishments of an enterprise of the other state if they act for the enterprise in the ordinary course of their business. You would therefore look at similar rules as apply above in the UK's domestic law.

Summary

It is possible to trade in the UK via an agent and avoid UK corporation tax on the profits. However you'd need to ensure that you avoid the dependent agency provisions. The best way to do this is to use a professional agency company.

Alternatively you could form your own and keep control of the agency company separate from the principal. In particular if the agency could represent other principals this would be very persuasive evidence of independent agency status.

If this is not possible you should ensure that the transactions are undertaken as much on as arm's length basis as possible. Crucially, ensure you retain all documentation to support this.

Collecting tax from the offshore company

You might think that given the offshore principal is a non UK resident company, this would in any case put it outside the Revenue's clutches - as the practicalities of enforcing any debt against the offshore company may be more trouble that it's worth.

This may well be true, were it not for the existence of the agent. There are specific provisions in the tax legislation that provide a practical means of taxing a non-resident by imposing the liabilities and obligations under the Taxes Acts on the non-resident's 'UK representative'. Note that these provisions only apply where there is a charge on the non-resident in the first place. If there is no liability under the permanent establishment rules, these provisions can't apply.

The collection provisions then work by treating the tax obligations and liabilities of the non-resident as though they were additionally the obligations and liabilities of the UK representative. This provides a practical assessment and collection mechanism for non- residents.

What is a UK representative?

The tax legislation defines the 'UK representative' as:

"the permanent establishment through which a non -resident company or individual carries on a UK trade."

The collection provisions provide that any staff or other personnel acting in the UK branch or any agent acting for the non-resident would fulfill the representative role and be competent to be the non- resident's 'UK representative'. It doesn't matter what the title of the staff is or even whether they are employees or self employed.

It's also worth noting that a partner in a partnership can be the UK representative of a non-resident. This would occur where a non- resident trades in the UK though a UK partnership (of which he or she is not a member). In such circumstances, the partners in the UK partnership will be jointly liable, as UK representative, for the tax payable by the non-resident.

This means that anyone (e.g. a manager, agent etc.) could be classed as the UK representative and be liable for the UK income tax liability.

Where the UK representative is liable to UK tax they'll be given a separate tax reference number to account for their tax liabilities in their capacity as the agent of the non-resident.

Dependent v Independent agents

It's clear from the above that UK agents can and often will be UK representatives for the purposes of the collection provisions.

However HMRC make a distinction between dependent and independent agents. Independent agents are not required to provide information to the extent that it is not practical for them to do so having acted to the best of their knowledge and belief after taking all reasonable steps to obtain the information.

To qualify as an independent agent the agent and its principal must be independent businesses dealing at arm's length.

Independent agents are also given the statutory right to be indemnified from the non-resident trader. As a matter of practice though the UK agent would be well advised to seek contractual indemnity from the non-residents to ensure it's enforceable overseas.

Exemptions from being a UK representative

The tax legislation states that the following can't be UK representatives for income tax and capital gains tax:

- Agents who are not regular agents. In general if a non- resident is trading in the UK through an agent that agent should be regarded as a regular agent.

The key distinction is between '...casual employment, temporary employment, for a transaction or few transactions, and regular appointment of a permanent agent who is there as representing the foreigner...'

- Brokers, investment managers and members' agents and managing agents of syndicates at

What income is the UK agent taxed on?

The UK agent is fully taxed on the profits of the trade carried out by the UK branch. In terms of other investment income though the tax liability for the non-resident on UK investment income is principally through deduction at source. As the tax rules limit the tax in such circumstances to the tax, if any, deducted at source there would be no need to assess a UK agent on the non-resident's UK investment income.

Remember that these provisions only apply where there is a UK representative. If any UK activities are carried out with no UK agents or other individuals it's unlikely HMRC could raise any assessments for UK tax.

Chapter 14

Tax Checklist: Using An Offshore Company

Offshore Tax Checklist

Using an Offshore Company to Reduce Tax

Yes	No	
		Consider your residence and domicile status both now and in the future. This may be crucial, particularly if you're looking to avoid capital gains tax on a disposal of assets held in the company.
		Consider what you want the company for. Will it be an overseas investment company (e.g. holding let property), a trading company carrying out an overseas trade or for asset protection purposes?
		Will the company be owned directly by you, or will it be a subsidiary of another company (UK or Overseas)?
		If you control any other companies the new offshore company will be 'associated' for tax purposes. This means that the tax bands applicable to the UK company (and the overseas company if it is subject to UK corporation tax) will be reduced - potentially increasing the corporation tax charge for the UK company.

Offshore Tax Checklist

Using an Offshore Company to Reduce Tax

Yes	No	
		Can you establish central management and control overseas? If you can't the company will just be treated as another UK resident company. This eliminates the benefits of offshore status and the company would then be charged to UK tax on its worldwide income and gains. Overseas directors would be required so you'd need to appoint these and ensure they actually run the business.
		Will you be holding the shares? If you're UK resident you can do this but you would need to ensure that the overseas directors actually run the company and weren't just 'rubber stamping' your decisions. If you want to use a trust to own the shares get this established and settle the shares to the trust.
		Consider how you'll be financing the company. The company will presumably need assets or cash, so you need to ascertain whether you'll loan funds to the company or subscribe for shares. In tax terms debt is often preferred as interest may be tax deductible, however you may need to consider transfer pricing and thin capitalisation requirements that prevent the company being financed with too much debt.
		What UK taxes are you looking to avoid or reduce? Tax on income, Tax on Capital Gains or Inheritance tax?

Offshore Tax Checklist

Using an Offshore Company to Reduce Tax

Yes	No	
		If you're looking to avoid tax on the income, your main concern here will be S720 ITA. Essentially unless you're a non-UK resident, a non-UK domiciliary or can show that the company was established for bona fide commercial reasons and not to avoid (UK) tax, the income of the offshore company can be taxed on you in the UK.
		If you're looking at avoiding UK tax on any capital gain you'll be faced with S13 TCGA and S731 ITA . These can tax any capital gain on you in the UK. However if you are a non-UK domiciliary, you can establish the company was set up for clear commercial reasons or could plan to be non-resident for a future disposal you may be able to avoid CGT on the disposal by the company.
		If you're avoiding Inheritance tax, the key issue will be your domicile status. As a non-UK domiciliary you can hold UK assets via an offshore company and ensure they're excluded from your UK estate for inheritance tax purposes. Watch out for the 17 year rule though. If you're UK resident for at least 17 of the previous 20 years you'll be a deemed domiciliary and subject to Inheritance tax on the offshore company shares.

Offshore Tax Checklist

Using an Offshore Company to Reduce Tax

Yes	No	
		Review any double tax treaty. Crucially you'll be looking at the residence article as well as the business profits and capital gains articles. Your aim here will be to assess which country trading income and capital gains will be assessed in.
		Remember that any income extracted from the offshore company to the UK will be subject to UK income tax.(Unless you're a non-UK domiciliary - in which case you can avoid income tax by retaining income overseas).
		Last but certainly not least - ensure the overseas tax and company regime is reviewed in detail.

Part II
Tax Planning With Offshore Trusts

Chapter 15

Introduction

Many people are interested in using offshore trusts to both protect their assets as well as minimising their tax liabilities.

Offshore trusts were traditionally popular in the 1980s but there have been a number of anti avoidance rules that have been specifically targeted at these structures. Their aim is to reduce the opportunities to use these to reduce UK taxes.

Nevertheless, there are still opportunities available, and this guide will look at:

- How offshore trusts are taxed, and

- What opportunities remain to use offshore trusts tax efficiently.

For instance, there are numerous opportunities for non doms to use offshore trusts (as well as offshore companies) given their privileged tax status.

In addition, although the capital gains tax avoidance rules are very wide in scope and significantly limit the use of offshore trusts for CGT avoidance in many cases, the income tax rules are less restrictive. There can therefore be opportunities to use offshore trusts as a shelter for foreign income.

We look at all of this, and much more in this part of the book.

Chapter 16

How Offshore Trusts Are Taxed

What is an offshore trust?

An offshore trust is a legal entity into which you can pass ownership and control of your assets. The assets are then managed by a trustee (such as a trusted firm of accountants or lawyers) in the interests of the beneficiaries (your family for example). The person who puts the assets into the trust (the settlor) may have a variety of reasons for distancing himself or herself from the ownership of the assets. For example, to remain anonymous for personal or business purposes or to avoid tax.

Offshore trusts are usually set up in tax havens or low tax jurisdictions such as the Channel Islands.

Please note that you should only consider using offshore trusts (and other offshore structures) after receiving advice from a qualified professional who fully understands your personal circumstances.

When is a trust non-resident?

A trust currently counts as non-resident for both income tax and capital gains tax purposes if all of the trustees are non-resident and the general administration of the trust is carried out abroad. However from April 6, 2007, a trust would only be non-resident if either all the trustees were non-resident, or if some of the trustees were non-resident and the settlor was non-UK domiciled and resident when the trust was set up.

As the trust is non-resident it is not usually subject to capital gains tax in respect of UK or overseas assets (in other words, the same as an individual). Subject to anti-avoidance legislation, offshore trusts are therefore capable of sheltering both UK and foreign capital gains.

Income Tax

Non-residents are not subject to UK tax on foreign income and therefore, in the absence of anti-avoidance legislation, offshore trusts can shelter such income. However, trusts are subject to income tax if the source of the income is the UK (just as an individual would be). Different trusts pay tax at different rates, although the type of trust most likely to be used in offshore tax planning would be a discretionary trust.

These trusts would pay tax at an effective 30.55% on UK dividends and 45% on other income or gains for 2013/2014.

Capital Gains Tax

The disposal of assets into a trust is a chargeable disposal for capital gains tax purposes and therefore a capital gain would arise. As the settlor is deemed to be 'connected' with the trust, any proceeds would be deemed to be equivalent to the market value of the assets transferred, it would therefore not be possible to avoid capital gains tax by simply gifting the assets.

The most effective method of establishing a trust from a capital gains tax perspective would therefore be to invest cash and let the trustees use this to invest as they see fit (in accordance with the trust deed). As the asset gifted is cash it falls outside the scope of capital gains tax.

Another possibility would be to settle assets that have a low initial value but which are expected to show significant growth in value. For example, shares in a newly formed company. Any growth in the value of the shares would occur offshore and, subject to the anti-avoidance rules, be outside the scope of UK capital gains tax.

Example:

Bert is considering purchasing a share in a small South African mining company for £50,000. He is hoping that the mine will strike gold and the shares will rocket in value. Rather than purchase the shares in his own name, he goes to see his solicitor and forms an offshore trust into which he settles the

£50,000. The trust then purchases the shares in the South African company. Any increase in value of the company would be effectively tax free as the trust would be outside the scope of UK capital gains tax. However, as we shall see, matters are not always that simple.

Inheritance Tax

A trust is subject to UK inheritance tax if the settlor was domiciled or deemed to be domiciled in the UK when he set up the trust.

Example:

Petro is of Italian domicile and has moved to Britain to expand his business into the UK. He has substantial assets in Italy and wishes to protect these from inheritance tax. If Petro sets up an offshore trust, provided he is not UK domiciled at the date of creation, the overseas assets will be outside the scope of UK inheritance tax, irrespective of the fact that Petro may later acquire a UK domicile.

The problem with an offshore discretionary trust is that it can lead to a large inheritance tax cost for a UK domiciled individual (non-UK domiciliaries are considered later in the guide).

A transfer of assets to a discretionary trust is called a chargeable lifetime transfer (CLT). This means that a proportion of inheritance tax is paid during the settlor's lifetime.

There are a number of complex rules governing this area. However, in essence the available nil rate band remaining is deducted from the value of the gift (in other words, the assets transferred into the trust) and tax is payable at 20% or 25% depending on whether the trust or the settlor is to pay the tax.

There is also a regime for taxing the assets of the trust. This is necessary, as when you transfer assets into a discretionary trust they are taken out of your estate and are therefore not subject to inheritance tax along with other assets you own.

The inheritance tax consequences of transferring to a discretionary trust are not straightforward and the calculation is pretty complex. What happens is that an effective rate of IHT is calculated based on the initial value of the trust (taking into account previous transfers and all relief) based on IHT payable at 6%.

Then when assets are distributed out of the trust, and on every tenth anniversary of the date the trust is set up, inheritance tax is payable on the amount distributed or the trust assets. This ensures that the trust is subject to a form of inheritance tax.

In summary, there are two main circumstances where a discretionary trust is free of inheritance tax:

- Where the trust is within the settlor's nil rate band and remains within the nil rate band for the following 10 anniversaries. The key problem with this trust is that its value is limited to the amount of the nil rate band (£325,000 for the 2013/2014 tax year).

One possible plan could be to use the trust as a holding device in which the value of funds initially settled is low and then perhaps distribute the funds before the trust's 10th anniversary. The benefit of this is that for an exit before the first 10-year anniversary, the rate of inheritance tax is based on the value of funds when the trust was created. In this case there would be no inheritance tax exit charge.

- Where the assets transferred into the trust are covered by an inheritance tax exemption such as Business Property Relief (BPR). This relief provides for a full or partial exemption from inheritance tax where 'business assets' are gifted. Typical business assets include assets used in a trade, shares in unquoted trading companies and certain commercial property. There are a number of other conditions that would need to be satisfied to successfully claim Business Property Relief.

There are therefore a number of potential tax advantages from using an offshore trust.

However, the key drawback for many will be how the anti avoidance rules impact on them.

Anti Avoidance Rules

There are two principal obstacles that anyone planning to use an offshore trust has to overcome to shelter their income and gains through an offshore trust:

- Tax anti-avoidance legislation which attributes *income* to the settlor. The income of an offshore trust is assessable as the settlor's if the actual or potential beneficiaries include him, his spouse or minor children or if any of them receives a benefit.

- Anti-avoidance legislation which attributes *gains* to the settlor. The provisions attribute gains to the settlor where any 'defined persons' are actual or potential beneficiaries who receive a benefit from the trust. The term 'defined person' includes the settlor and his spouse, their children, their children's spouses, their grandchildren and their grandchildren's spouses. Clearly this is a particularly wide anti-avoidance provision (and is much wider than the definition for UK trusts, which only applies to the settlor, his spouse and his minor children).

Chapter 17

The Offshore Trust Anti Avoidance Rules - Income Tax

As we've seen in the previous chapter, there are some significant benefits, however just to recap you're looking at the following:

- No UK tax on overseas income
- No UK tax on any gains made (either in the UK or offshore)
- No UK IHT in certain circumstances

So in other words an offshore trust could invest in Bulgarian property with no UK taxes on overseas rental income or any CGT on a future disposal.

Given that UK taxes could knock out 50% of your returns this is a pretty big incentive. There are also other benefits such as increased privacy and ring fencing assets offshore away from potential creditors.

Of course, its not quite as simple as setting up an offshore trust to hold your foreign assets if you want to be able to get the benefit of these tax advantages.

HMRC has a number of anti avoidance rules that they can use to prevent you from enjoying these tax benefits.

How do the anti avoidance rules work?

There are a number of anti avoidance rules which apply to offshore trusts. We've seen in the first part of the book, the various rules that apply to offshore companies. In many cases the same rules will apply to UK residents using offshore trusts.

In terms of income tax, the key provisions are in S720-731 ITA 2007, which provide for wide-ranging anti-avoidance powers designed to prevent the avoidance of Income Tax by individuals using offshore trusts (and companies).

The conditions for application of Section 720 and S727 are:

There must be a transfer of assets by an individual

- As a result of the transfer income becomes payable to a non-resident person.
- The transferor must have power to enjoy that income in some way, or receive/be entitled to receive a capital sum.
- The transferor must be ordinarily resident in the UK in the year of liability.

If all of these conditions are fulfilled, the income which becomes payable to the offshore trust is deemed to be that of the individual who made the transfer, to the extent he has power to enjoy that income.

The first point to consider would be whether there would be a 'transfer of assets' by you. The UK tax authorities take a wide view of what constitutes a transfer of assets.

For example S720 may apply:

- where an individual transfers cash to establish a non- resident trust, or
- subscribes for the share capital of an offshore company, or
- where an individual transfers assets such as shares or property to a new or existing non-resident trust or other person abroad.

It can also apply where intangible assets are transferred; for example a UK individual may transfer his services to an offshore company or trust.

The view of the Revenue is that a transfer may be made by way of sale or purchase of assets, or by way of gift.

However, one problem is that S720 doesn't just apply where an individual transfers assets, rather it applies where an individual either transfers, or is associated with the transfer of assets. In particular, if the operations were contemplated as a single scheme they could be associated.

What constitutes an associated operation is complex, and is essentially a factual matter, however the legislation states that this includes:

'... an operation of any kind effected by any person in relation to any of the assets transferred or any assets representing, whether directly or indirectly, any of the assets transferred, or to the income arising from any such assets, or to any assets representing, whether directly or indirectly, the accumulations of income arising from any such assets...'

It's therefore given an incredibly wide scope to essentially include any actions undertaken by you in relation to the trust assets in connection with the generation of income arising to the trust.

It's also worthwhile noting that associated operations can also have separate Inheritance tax consequences and in this case the Revenue define associated operations as two or more dispositions, of which:

- one is effected with reference to the other or
- one is effected with a view to enabling the other to be effected or
- one facilitates the effecting of the other.

Whilst the Inheritance tax definition is not directly relevant, it does give a good indication of the underlying purpose of the associated operation rule.

On the basis that the conditions above were satisfied, any income arising to the non-resident trust can be taxed by S720, whether UK source income or foreign source income.

Note that one of the above conditions is that the UK resident must have power to enjoy the income arising to the non-resident (e.g. as a shareholder of an overseas company or as a beneficiary of a non-resident trust). Even if you did not actually receive any income from the trust it is the potential to enjoy the income that is important. As such you would have to not receive any of the income at all (and have no potential right under the terms of the trust) to avoid the income being taxed on you.

The alternative provision is S731.

This applies where assets have been transferred abroad and a UK resident other than the settlor obtains a benefit. In order for this to apply the following conditions would need to be satisfied:

- There must be a transfer of assets.
- As a result of which (alone or in conjunction with associated operations) income becomes payable to a non-resident person.
- As a result of the transfer, an individual other than the transferor receives a benefit, which is not otherwise chargeable to Income Tax.
- The recipient of the benefit must be ordinarily resident in the UK in the year of charge.

Section 731 is different from S720 and S727 in that it taxes non-transferors on benefits received.

Benefits chargeable by Section 731 include payments of any kind, for example cash (capital distributions), the use of property (e.g. rent free occupation of a house), interest free loans, etc. Where the conditions are satisfied, the individual receiving the benefit is liable to tax on the amount or value of the benefit, (although the charge can be limited by the amount of past or future available 'relevant income' of the trust - see below).

It's also worth bearing in mind that Section 731 charges the amount or value of the benefit received to the extent that it is matched by the available relevant income of the offshore trust or company.

'Relevant' income for this purpose means income that arises to the offshore trust or company which can be used to provide a benefit for the beneficiary concerned. Income is only taken into account once for this purpose. Therefore rental income, for instance, received by the trust and held in the trust would be treated as relevant income for this purposes.

If there is any relevant income in the trust and a capital distribution is made, the capital distribution could be taxed on the UK resident beneficiary as income to the extent of the relevant income.

TAX PLANNING WITH OFFSHORE COMPANIES & TRUSTS | 103

Even if there is a liability under S720 - S731 what impact would this have?

Where the provisions apply this would deem the income or benefit to arise to the UK individual and would therefore be subject to UK income tax. S720-S731 applies unless you can show that the exemption in S733 onwards applies.

In order for this to apply you would need to demonstrate either condition A or condition B is satisfied:

Condition A

It would not be reasonable to draw the conclusion, from all the circumstances of the case, that the purpose of avoiding liability to taxation was the purpose, or one of the purposes, for which the relevant transactions or any of them were effected.

Condition B

All the relevant transactions were genuine commercial transactions. It would not be reasonable to draw the conclusion, from all the circumstances of the case, that any one or more of those transactions was more than incidentally designed for the purpose of avoiding liability to taxation.

Actually persuading the Revenue that you can take advantage of this exemption can in practice be difficult.

S720 and S731 are essentially the main income tax avoidance rules and will catch many UK residents looking to use an offshore trust unless you can take advantage of the exemption or minimise the deemed income to an acceptable level.

The other main exception to these rules is that non UK domiciliaries would only be caught if the income was remitted to the UK. Therefore these anti avoidance rules do not cause a significant problem for most non UK doms. We'll look at these shortly.

The above applies just for the purposes of UK income tax. There are a whole lot of separate CGT provisions designed to catch UK residents who use offshore trusts to dispose of assets free of UK taxes. We'll look at these in the next chapter.

2013 changes to the anti avoidance rules

As we've seen above, there is a general motive exemption which prevents liability arising in circumstances where the transactions were not motivated by tax avoidance or were commercial transactions only incidentally motivated by tax avoidance.

However, the exemption is relatively narrow and the European Commission have argued that the provisions breach the EU freedoms of establishment and movement of capital.

The 2013 changes seek to bring the legislation into compliance with EU law and also to provide clarity in some areas of practical application of the provisions. The main changes are as follows:

- A new exemption for situations where the imposition of UK tax liability would constitute an unjustified and disproportionate restriction of the individual's freedom of establishment or movement of capital in EU law. The exemption is restricted to genuine commercial business activities overseas and also transactions which do not involve commercial activities but are nevertheless genuine transactions protected by the single market.

Business transactions will not be regarded as "genuine" unless they are on arm's length terms and give rise to income attributable to economically significant activity that takes place overseas. "Brass plate" companies would not be regarded as economically significant for this purpose.

- It will be made clearer that double tax agreements do not override these provisions.

- Other changes will clarify the way in which income is matched with benefits received by an individual in circumstances where an individual other than the original transferor is the chargeable person.

These changes take effect from Royal Assent to Finance Bill 2013 but with retrospective effect from 6 April 2012.

The new exemption is clearly broader than the existing commercial transactions exemption as it applies even where transactions are motivated by tax avoidance, provided they are genuine.

Chapter 18

The Offshore Trust Anti Avoidance Rules - Capital Gains Tax

There are two main ways that CGT anti avoidance rules can apply to offshore trusts:

Firstly, settlors of offshore trusts can be attributed capital gains of that trust, and

Secondly, beneficiaries of offshore trusts who actually receive capital payments/distributions from the trust can be taxed on the capital gains of that trust.

Tax charge on settlors

This provision attributes capital gains to the settlor of a trust if defined people are actual or potential beneficiaries or receive a benefit.

Defined people include the settlor and his spouse, their children and their children's spouses and their grandchildren and their grandchildren's spouses.

It can also include a company controlled by the settlor or one or more of the "defined people") or a company associated with a company controlled by the settlor/the defined people.

These gains are treated as forming the highest part of the amount on which the settlor is charged to CGT in the year (usually 28%).

This is the most far reaching definition aimed at trusts as the other anti avoidance rules only target cases where the settlor and his spouse could benefit.

This means that a newly formed offshore trust would only operate as a CGT shelter if the settlor, his spouse and grandchildren (and their spouses) are excluded from the trust.

Tax charge on beneficiaries

These provisions catch gains realised by the offshore trust which are not assessed as the settlors under the above rules.

How this works

In each tax year, the non-resident trust should make an assessment of its trust gains for the year. These are then treated as accruing to beneficiaries who receive capital payments in that year.

They may also be treated as accruing to beneficiaries who have received capital payments in an earlier year, but only insofar as those payments have not already been taxed by reference to earlier trust gains.

If the trust gains exceed the current and past capital payments they are simply carried forward.

So the main effect of the above is to treat trust gains as the gains of beneficiaries, but only when they actually receive benefits from the trust (i.e. a form of remittance basis)

A "Capital Payment" for this purpose has a very wide meaning and doesn't just apply to a transfer of cash from an offshore trust. It includes the transfer of assets from the offshore trust as well as the conferring of a benefit.

Therefore capital payments will also include interest free/low interest loans from the trust as well as occupation of trust property at a below market rental.

There are also provisions that apply an additional ("supplementary") charge for beneficiaries who are UK-resident and/or ordinarily resident.

The aim of the supplementary charge is to charge an additional tax charge when the capital payments are matched with gains from earlier tax years.

The effect of this additional charge is to make the highest effective tax rate 28.8% for a basic rate taxpayer and 44.8% for a higher rate taxpayer.

There is no supplementary charge where gains are matched to capital payments made:

(i) in tax years prior to the tax year in which the gain is realised;
(ii) in the tax year the gain is realised; or
(iii) in the tax year following the tax year in which the gain is realised.

2013 Changes

The European Commission takes the view that the above anti avoidance rules are a disproportionate infringement of the EU freedom of establishment and free movement of capital. As such HMRC have proposed some amendments to bring section 13 into conformity with EU law. The main changes are as follows:

- Introduction of a new exemption which excludes gains from "economically significant" activity carried on outside the UK, broadly the provisions of goods or services on a commercial basis involving the use of staff, premises, equipment and addition of economic value commensurate with the size and nature of those activities.

- A general motive exemption for gains on disposals where neither the disposal of the asset nor the acquisition or holding of the asset by the non-UK company formed part of a scheme or arrangements to avoid capital gains tax or corporation tax. This exemption is not restricted to trading companies so should protect investment holding companies set up for reasons other than UK tax avoidance, for example a local company set up to acquire foreign real estate.

- The participation threshold for attribution of gains will be increased from over 10% to over 25%.

The changes will take effect from Royal Assent to Finance Bill 2013 but with retrospective effect from 6 April 2012.

Chapter 19

Summary Of Tax Treatment For Offshore Trust/Beneficiaries

As there are a lot of overlapping provisions it's useful to summarise exactly what we've covered in the first few chapters:

Tax Treatment of Offshore Trusts

The trust itself

Providing the trust is established as a non-resident trust it will be exempt from UK capital gains tax and also UK income tax on overseas income. This therefore makes an offshore trust potentially very attractive in terms of avoiding UK tax. As such there are pretty comprehensive anti avoidance rules that apply to tax settlors of such trusts or beneficiaries.

If you're setting up an offshore trust

You will be classed as a 'settlor' of the trust. This has a number of implications.

Firstly if you're a UK domiciliary you will be taxed on any gains that the trust realises if you or your close family can benefit. So if the trust sells a property at a gain of £1,000,000, although the trust itself will be exempt from tax on the gain, you would be taxed on the gain arising.

This doesn't apply though if you're a non UK domiciliary as the 2008 Finance Bill preserved the exception for non UK domiciliary.

Secondly there are the transfer of asset rules to consider.

The legislation imposes an income tax on individuals ordinarily resident in the UK in three broad circumstances:-

- under section 720 ITA, where they have power to enjoy income which arises to an offshore trust where the income arises as a result of a transfer of assets and/or associated operations;

- under section 727, where they receive or are entitled to receive capital sums as a result of a transfer of assets and/or associated operations, which have resulted in income arising to an offshore trust;

- under section 731, where they receive a benefit provided out of assets available for the purpose as a result of a transfer of assets and/or associated operations, which have resulted in income arising to an offshore trust.

Therefore anyone who established an offshore trust and transferred assets to it could easily find themselves taxed on any income arising if they can derive a benefit from the trust.

There is, though, a key exception to this if the trust was established without a tax avoidance motive.

These transfer of asset provisions also apply to non UK domiciliaries albeit in an amended form. The broad aim is to tax them on the same basis as if they'd owned the assets personally and therefore if they are entitled to use the remittance basis of tax (in other words if they either make a claim or are entitled due to the £2,000 de minimis limit for unremitted overseas income and gains) they are subject to the remittance basis on the offshore trust income.

Essentially therefore if the offshore trust income is non UK income it would be subject to the remittance basis and, provided it was not remitted by the settlor (or any benefits etc. weren't received in the UK), there should be no UK tax on the settlor.

If, though, the asset owned by the offshore trust was a UK asset the remittance basis wouldn't apply and the non dom would be taxed on the trust income whether retained overseas or not.

TAX PLANNING WITH OFFSHORE COMPANIES & TRUSTS | 111

If you're a beneficiary

If you're a beneficiary of an offshore trust (which can also apply to settlors) not only can you be taxed on any benefits that you derive from the trust under the above anti avoidance rules, but you will also be taxed on any capital gains of the trust if you receive capital payments from the trust.

This is an area that has been subject to a lot of discussion over the past few months; however in essence it's pretty straightforward.

Any UK resident and domiciled beneficiaries of offshore trusts are taxed on any capital gains of the trust if they receive capital payments from the trust. The trustees need to keep a track of capital payments and gains to ensure that they are accurately matched and gains can, for example, be carried forward if current capital payments are not high enough which will then allocate the gains to future capital payments.

Non UK domiciliaries who are beneficiaries of offshore trusts are now also within the scope of these provisions. This means that gains of the offshore trust can be charged on UK beneficiaries when they receive capital payments.

Note that this applies whether the trust has UK or overseas assets.

However as for the transfer of asset provisions above there are specific exemptions for non UK domiciliaries entitled to use the remittance basis. In particular the remittance basis will apply to the capital gains of the trust; again irrespective of whether the gains arise from overseas or UK assets. As such, provided the capital payments are retained outside the UK, tax could be avoided.

Chapter 20

UK Protectors & Offshore Trusts

Protectors are often part and parcel of an offshore trust package and they can provide valuable comfort to the trust settlor (i.e. the person who establishes the trust) that their wishes and the wishes of the beneficiaries are being taken into account.

The protector can also act as a liaison between the beneficiaries and the trustees to resolve any disputes which may arise from time to time.

Difference between a trustee and protector

The protector does not have the same powers as the trustee. In particular the legal ownership of the trust property is held by the trustee who is responsible for the management and control of the trust and its property. The protector, however, is not the registered or legal owner of the trust property and would not be involved with the day to day administration of the Trust. He will have to fulfil certain duties and responsibilities and will also be given certain powers under the terms of the trust deed.

Why appoint a protector?

Usually a settlor would appoint a protector to ensure that the trustees exercise their powers and duties in a satisfactory manner.

Protectors can therefore provide an additional layer of security for the settlor in ensuring that any matters referred to in their letter of wishes are adhered to.

Usual powers of the protector

Any powers that are given to the Protector are provided for in the trust deed.

However, typical powers would be to appoint/remove trustees and beneficiaries. They could also be given wider powers to veto investment recommendations or distributions.

UK tax and Protectors

A key concern for many establishing offshore trusts is that they want to ensure that all of the trustees are non UK resident. The question is therefore whether having a UK resident Protector could make the trust UK resident. The rules relating to the residence of trusts are as follows:

- A trust will be UK resident if all the Trustees are resident in the UK;

- A trust will be non-UK resident if all the Trustees are resident outside the UK;

- If one or more of the Trustees is resident in the UK and the other or others are not, the residence of the trust will depend on the status of the settlor at the "relevant time".

- If, at the "relevant time", the settlor was resident, ordinarily resident and domiciled outside the UK then the trust will be a non-UK resident trust. Otherwise it will be a UK resident trust.

The residence of a trust can be crucial as if it's non UK resident it will generally be outside the scope of income tax and CGT on most income/capital gains.

Therefore would a UK resident protector make an offshore trust UK resident if all of the trustees were non resident?

This is very unlikely. It would need to be assessed whether the protector could be classed as a trustee for tax purposes. Given that the trust property is not vested in him and provided he does not have power to actually initiate action (only the power to veto proposals put forward by the actual trustees) the Protector shouldn't be a trustee.

To support this any settlor should however ensure that the actual trustees have a free reign over how to invest income & capital and also how to distribute income. The role of the Protector should therefore be retained to veto appointments or to veto large capital distributions.

This should assist in demonstrating that any UK resident Protectors would not cause an offshore trust to be UK resident.

Chapter 21

UK Tax For Offshore Life Interest Trusts

Most offshore trusts established now will be discretionary trusts. However, during the 1990's offshore life interest trusts were very common. Life interest trusts are effectively the same as an interest in possession trust with the life tenants being entitled to the income of the trust and the capital being held for other individuals (known as the remaindermen).

In this chapter we look at the tax treatment of offshore life interest trusts where the beneficiaries are looking to leave the UK and establish residence and domicile overseas. In particular we look at whether the life interest trust can be wound up and the assets transferred to the non-resident beneficiaries.

Before 22 March 2006, all life interest trusts were treated for inheritance tax purposes as though they were owned by the beneficiary with the life interest (called the life tenant).

Therefore if the life tenants were UK domiciled (either in general law or under the deemed domicile provisions) then they should be within the scope of UK IHT on their worldwide assets.

The trust regime underwent a number of changes in 2006 and 2008.

Most trusts are now treated as relevant property trusts and taxed like discretionary trusts. However there is in exception for life interest trusts created before 22 March 2006 where the pre-2006 beneficiaries remain in place or were changed before 6 October 2008.

These life interest trusts will not fall into the 'relevant property trust' tax regime until the current interest in possession ('IIP') ends. If the IIP ends and the assets of the trust pass to another individual absolutely, the old rules apply and there may be a potentially exempt transfer (and therefore subject to the 7 year survivorship period).

If the IIP ends and the assets stay in the trust, then the assets are included in the estate of the life tenant if the IIP ended on their death (and assets re-based at death value for CGT purposes); if the IIP ended during their lifetime, then the assets are treated as a chargeable lifetime transfer to the 'new trust' (with a lifetime charge to IHT if they're UK deemed domiciled).

The new trust would be treated as a discretionary trust and 10-yearly charges and exit charges will then start to apply.

The termination of an IIP will also now be treated as a gift from the point of view of the gift with reservation rules. So if a trust is changed to a full discretionary trust, with the life tenant retaining any entitlement to benefit, this would be treated as a gift with reservation of benefit and the trust assets would still be treated as part of the life tenant's estate for IHT purposes.

In terms of CGT if a trust beneficiary was to become absolutely entitled to the assets during his lifetime, this would be a deemed disposal by the trustees at market value and they would be responsible for paying any CGT liability arising as a result. However if the trust is non-resident and the beneficiary is non- resident there should be no UK CGT liability in any case. There are a number of anti avoidance rules which apply in particular S80 IHTA 1984 which states:

'...80.-(1) Where a settlor or his spouse is beneficially entitled to an interest in possession in property immediately after it becomes comprised in the settlement, the property shall for the purposes of this Chapter be treated as not having become comprised in the settlement on that occasion; but when the property or any part of it becomes held on trusts under which neither of those persons is beneficially entitled to an interest in possession, the property or part shall for those purposes be treated as becoming comprised in a separate settlement made by that one of them who ceased (or last ceased) to be beneficially entitled to an interest in possession in it...'

Essentially this is stating that if the trust gave the settlor or spouse an initial life interest, then the status of the trust will be re-tested by reference to the

TAX PLANNING WITH OFFSHORE COMPANIES & TRUSTS | 117

domicile of the settlor/spouse when their interest comes to an end. If they are UK domiciled or deemed domiciled at that time all assets will become subject to the discretionary trust regime.

Therefore if the life interest ends and the trust continues, if they are UK deemed domiciled, the trust could not be an excluded property trust and would be subject to the relevant UK inheritance tax regime. This would clearly not be desirable.

If, though, the trust was terminated and the assets transferred to the beneficiaries this should not apply as there is no continuing trust.

Once they've lost UK residence and UK deemed domicile status they could then establish an offshore discretionary trust which could be exempt from UK inheritance tax on a future return to the UK.

Therefore, in terms of UK tax, if the trust beneficiaries are leaving the UK although they may still be deemed UK domiciliaries it should be possible to transfer the trust assets to them personally without there being an immediate charge to UK inheritance tax. CGT should also not be an issue if they are non UK resident.

Chapter 22

Migrating a UK Trust Overseas

Trust migration essentially means that a UK resident trust becomes non UK resident.

There are a couple of different ways that this could happen.

How does a trust migrate?

- Firstly, if the UK trustees moved abroad and become non UK resident the trust itself would also then become non UK resident.

- Secondly, (and the more likely scenario) the UK resident trustees retire and non-resident trustees are appointed in their place. This then also makes the trust non- resident.

Why would a trust migrate?

There are a number of reasons why a trust may migrate. However, these are tied in with the benefits of being non UK resident, which we've looked at in previous chapters.

Some of the key UK tax planning reasons include:

- Any overseas income would be free of UK income tax
- Capital gains would be exempt from UK capital gains tax
- UK source income would be subject to the excluded income rules so that interest and dividends could be free of UK tax.

Note, though, that the excluded income rules contain an exemption where the income arises to a trust which has a UK beneficiary. Therefore if there were UK beneficiaries you may find that UK income tax was still due by the trust on foreign income.

Tax on migration

When a trust migrates the trustees are deemed to have sold and immediately reacquired all the trust property at its market value. This then ensures that any gains on assets held by the trustees accrue (and are taxed) before the trust becomes non UK resident (and outside the scope of UK CGT).

Note though that there is an exemption from this migration charge for UK situated assets that are assets of a trade carried on in the UK by the trustees.

Other CGT consequences of migration

Capital gains in the tax year of migration

As for individuals any capital gains that arise on disposals in the same tax year as migration are fully charged to CGT even if actually after the migration.

Capital payments

As we've seen in chapter 6 one of the anti avoidance rules attributes capital gains of non- resident/offshore trusts on UK beneficiaries that receive capital payments/distributions from the trust. Capital gains in the offshore trust can also be allocated against unallocated capital payments from earlier years.

When a trust migrates it should be borne in mind that a capital payment is brought into account for this purpose even if it was received when the trust was resident.

In addition a beneficiary of the trust is taxed even if the trust is a single trust split into smaller funds and the capital gain arises in a fund from which he is excluded.

The net effect of this is that a UK beneficiary who is paid out in full in the year before the trust migrates can be taxed in full on subsequent trust gains even though he/she can't benefit from them.

When should a trust migrate?

Taking all of the above into account exactly when should a trust migrate? It has to be said that the migration of trusts is not too common. The big drawback of course is the deemed disposal for CGT purposes on migration. This makes trust migration beneficial in very limited situations. There are three key occasions when migration could be tax efficient:

The main case when migrating a trust may be beneficial for tax purposes is where the trust assets don't have any latent capital gains (i.e. no deemed tax CGT charge on migration) and future capital gains won't be attributed to the settlor where the trust is non- resident. This will generally apply when a settlor is dead or a non dom.

In this scenario migration could be advisable as it could avoid UK tax on both capital gains and foreign income. Note, though, if there were UK resident and domiciled beneficiaries, making capital payments to them could negate the benefits.

Secondly, if the trust assets do show some latent capital gains but you're expecting much larger gains in the future. In this case the smaller tax charge on migration could be a good option to avoid the larger CGT in the future. The same rules apply as above, though, in terms of the trust not being a settlor interested trust.

Finally, if the trust assets show no latent capital gain and whilst the trust is currently settlor interested it won't be so in the future (e.g. if the settlor was to become non- resident in the future). If future gains are expected to be substantial a migration now may be a good option.

Chapter 23

Top Tax Planning Uses For Offshore Trusts

In this chapter we'll provide a summary of some of the top tax planning opportunities for offshore trusts.

The big advantage of an offshore trust is that, just like all non- residents it is exempt from UK tax on foreign income, and exempt from UK CGT (unless the assets sold are UK business assets). This could lead to massive tax planning advantages. The difficulties come in "side stepping" the anti avoidance rules that can tax UK settlors and beneficiaries on the trust income and capital gains.

Here are some of the top uses for offshore trusts:

- When the settlors/beneficiaries are non UK domiciliaries and claiming the remittance basis. They'll then be taxed on the income and (for beneficiaries) the capital gains of the trust on the remittance basis. Therefore income and gains can be retained overseas to avoid UK tax.

- When the settlor is a non dom but doesn't claim the remittance basis.

Here the offshore trust can be attractive in terms of avoiding CGT as the rule that attributes gains of offshore trusts to their UK settlors doesn't apply to non UK domiciliaries.

Therefore the trust can be used as a capital gain shelter.

- As a shelter for overseas income where the motive exemption applies.

Where there is a sound commercial reason for the use of the trust the anti avoidance rules that attribute income to UK settlors do not apply.

- Where the settlor is dead.

Clearly the rules attributing income and gains to the settlor cannot apply if he is dead. This could arise if a trust is formed under the terms of a will.

In this case the assets would secure a tax-free uplift in their base cost for capital gains tax purposes (as the assets would pass into the trust at the market value at the date of death). Of course the assets passing into the trust would be subject to any inheritance tax on death unless the value transferred falls within the nil rate band, or the assets are covered by any other inheritance tax reliefs (such as Business Property Relief).

Example

John's estate consisted of:

House	£250,000
Cash	£75,000
Shares	£500,000

On the assumption that the shares were in an unquoted trading company, they would qualify for Business Property Relief (BPR) and the inheritance tax position would be as follows:

House	£250,000
Cash	£75,000
Nil rate band -	£325,000
Shares	£500,000
BPR -	£500,000

Therefore the inheritance tax charge would be nil.

TAX PLANNING WITH OFFSHORE COMPANIES & TRUSTS | 123

Any subsequent gain arising on a disposal by John's heirs would be subject to UK capital gains tax (assuming the heirs are UK resident).

By contrast, John could have inserted a provision in his will for the shares to be settled in a non-resident discretionary trust. Inheritance tax would not be an issue, as the shares would qualify for BPR and, although John was a UK domiciliary, the anti-avoidance provisions should not apply as he is dead.

Assuming a subsequent disposal of the shares at a significant gain this would be outside the scope of UK capital gains tax as the gain would now be realised by a non-resident trust.

- As a CGT shelter where family are excluded

We'll look at this shortly. However as we've seen, the anti avoidance rules attribute capital gains to the settlor where beneficiaries include:

- the settlor
- his spouse
- their children and their spouses
- their grandchildren and their spouses

Therefore if an offshore trust was made by remote relations or friends of the beneficiaries they could be effective in avoiding capital gains tax being attributed to the settlor.

- As a foreign income shelter where you and your spouse are excluded from benefiting (e.g. a Children's or Grandchildren's settlement).

The anti avoidance rules that apply for income are much less stringent than capital gains. Therefore you could shelter foreign investment income in a trust for the benefit of your children.

- Where beneficiaries are or will be non-resident.

This then allows income and gains to be extracted free of UK tax.

Chapter 24

Using Offshore Trusts for CGT Avoidance

If you're interested in using offshore trusts for CGT avoidance the main problem you'll face are the anti avoidance rules that can attribute capital gains of offshore trusts back to UK settlors and beneficiaries.

As the trust is likely to be non UK resident the trust itself will be exempt from capital gains tax just as other non residents (e.g. companies and individuals) are. If it wasn't for the anti avoidance rules you could therefore use an offshore trust to hold property, financial investments or trading companies free of UK CGT.

In actual fact, though, through careful attention to the anti avoidance rules it's still possible to use offshore trusts for CGT avoidance.

The key occasions when you could still use an offshore trust for CGT avoidance are:

Settlements where the settlor is dead

The anti avoidance rules that attribute capital gains to the settlor won't apply if the settlor is dead. If the transfer to the trust is made on death an ancillary benefit to this is that any capital gain to the date of death is eliminated.

Any gains that arise in future to the trust would not then be attributed to the settlor. It would just be any beneficiaries that could be taxed (see below).

The main problem with leaving assets to an offshore trust in a will is that it will form part of the settlor estate for inheritance tax purposes. You may therefore be looking for transfer of assets that qualify for business property relief to eliminate inheritance tax (e.g. shares in unquoted trading companies).

Trusts with no family beneficiaries.

The anti avoidance rules attribute capital gains to the settlor where beneficiaries include:

- the settlor
- his spouse
- their children and their spouses
- their grandchildren and their spouses

Therefore if an offshore trust was made by remote relations or friends of the beneficiaries they could be effective in avoiding capital gains tax being attributed to the settlor.

A good option for this is to hold shares in newly formed trading companies.

The initial set up cost would be low and you could always ask a remote relation to set up the trust. You could also take advantage of the current low property prices and purchase bargain basement property via an offshore trust. Provided the set up was by remote relations any subsequent increase in value could be free of CGT if retained overseas.

You'd need to be careful to ensure that you weren't classed as the settlor if you were actually contributing to the trust in some way. If you could therefore get the friend/relation to settle funds on the trust out of their own funds this would avoid the problem. If there is some kind of reciprocal arrangement with you routing cash back to the friend to compensate them for the cost they incurred this could well be treated as you being the settlor.

To get a 'double whammy' in terms of tax benefits, if you can also ensure that the settlor is a non UK domiciliary, you could ensure that the trust is an excluded property trust (e.g. by using intermediate offshore holding companies) and therefore outside the scope of UK inheritance tax.

Setting up the trust

The best way of setting up the trust would be for the friend/relation to transfer cash to the trust. This is then free of CGT and allows the trustees to purchase shares/investments etc.

Benefiting from the trust

You can use the techniques above to avoid the anti avoidance rules and arrange disposals without this being taxed on you personally. But what if you wanted to benefit from the trust? Well, any distributions to you in the UK would be subject to UK tax if you're UK resident and domiciled.

The best bet is to extract from the trust as a non UK resident. You can then do so free of UK tax.

There are however other options. We look in later chapters of this guide at the tax implications of extracting cash from the trust.

Chapter 25

Offshore Trusts For Grandchildren

Offshore trusts for the benefit of grandchildren can be used to avoid income tax and CGT.

The opportunities for UK residents to successfully use offshore trusts to avoid UK tax have been significantly reduced over the past few years due to the scope of the anti avoidance rules in place.

These anti avoidance rules target both income and capital gains of the offshore trust.

The CGT avoidance rules covering offshore trusts are very wide in their scope.

One option to get around these rules could be to consider using a hybrid structure of an offshore company and trust.

In this case you would use a company resident in a country with which the UK has a suitable double tax treaty (such as Mauritius or Singapore).

You'd be looking at an offshore company owned by a UK resident shareholder and an offshore trust. The UK shareholder would have shares with a majority of the value but a minority of the votes, and the trust would have shares with a minority of the value but a majority of the votes.

This could then allow the gains in the company to be crystallised without the UK shareholder being attributed the gains.

In terms of the income of the company the anti avoidance rules aren't as wide and there are provisions to attribute income where the settlor, his spouse or minor children can benefit.

Therefore, ensuring that the offshore trust just benefits the grandchildren it should still be effective as a shelter from income tax.

The trust could have the income as a beneficiary without the income being attributed back to the individual who established the trust.

The next issue would be to ensure that the trust received the income (but not capital gains/receipts) and the MauritianCo did not receive the income (to prevent it being taxed on the settlor). One option here would be to use a partnership between the trust and the MauritianCo. Effectively they would sign a partnership agreement specifying an agreed profit and capital sharing ratio.

The income and any capital receipts would flow into the partnership which would then distribute the income and capital payments in accordance to the partnership agreement. Given the restrictions in various double tax treaties on which assets will qualify for the CGT exemption, this could be a good option for holding overseas investments.

This may therefore be a good option for a UK resident looking to make investments overseas. The capital gains could be effectively free of CGT and the income rolled up free of income tax for the benefit of the grandchildren.

Chapter 26

How Non Doms Can Use Offshore Trusts Even If They Don't Claim The Remittance Basis

Non UK domiciliaries are in a privileged position when it comes to UK tax.

In particular they have the option of claiming the remittance basis and being taxed on their foreign income and capital gains only when they actually bring the income or proceeds into the UK.

There are some drawbacks to claiming the remittance basis, (most notably a £30,000 or £50,000 tax charge once they have been UK resident for 8 or 12 tax years).

The alternative to claiming the remittance basis (and paying the £30,000/£50,000 charge) is just to opt to be taxed on the arising basis. This is the same way that most UK residents are taxed and means that foreign income and capital gains are taxed irrespective of whether the proceeds are retained abroad.

Using Offshore Trusts

In terms of using offshore trusts, if a non dom claims the remittance basis this will also usually apply to the income and gains that are attributed from the offshore trust under the anti avoidance rules. In practical terms this therefore means that a non dom can avoid UK tax on income and gains of an offshore trust by retaining the trust cash abroad if they claim the remittance basis.

What if they opt to be taxed on the arising basis?

There are still a number of benefits that non doms are entitled to - even if they claim the arising basis. Some of the key ones include:

- The inheritance tax advantages of non dom status if they've been resident for less than 17 years.
- The ability to retain overseas income or gains of £1,999 per tax year overseas and avoid UK tax on this.
- The flexibility to claim the remittance basis in the future if they wish (e.g. if there was large overseas income or capital gains.

All of these can be useful.

It's worth remembering that whilst the provisions relating to the use of offshore trusts by non doms have been tightened up, there is still one key exemption that allows non doms to use offshore trusts.

Settlor charge

S86 TCGA is one of the main trust anti avoidance rules and it applies 'settlor charge'. This means that the capital gains of an offshore trust are taxed directly on the UK resident trust settlor if the trust settlor or anyone on a list of 'defined people' can benefit. The list of defined people is pretty wide and includes the settlor, his spouse, their children and grandchildren.

So, anyone who transfers cash or other assets to an offshore trust will be taxed on capital gains of the trust if they or their family can benefit from the trust.

The reason for this is clear - an offshore trust that is non UK resident (i.e. it has non-resident trustees) will be exempt from UK capital gains tax on most assets. If this provision was not in place it would allow UK residents to own assets via an offshore trust and avoid CGT on the eventual disposal.

Whilst recent legislation has made a lot of changes for non doms, one thing that it doesn't really touch is this settlor charge.

This isn't just for non doms who are claiming the remittance basis -- but all non doms even if subject to the arising basis.

This is unusual as most of the anti avoidance rules now apply to non doms but in a special way (i.e. they apply the remittance basis where the non dom is subject to the remittance basis).

This means that a non dom could use an offshore trust to hold assets and benefit from the capital gains tax exemption in the trust. Effectively the trust could be a capital gains tax shelter.

Other provisions

You would however need to watch out for the other provisions which aren't as generous. In particular, there is S87 which applies a 'beneficiary charge'.

This applies a charge where beneficiaries receive capital payments from the trust. In this case it attributes gains of the trust to those capital payments.

However the key point is that it also applies to non doms. In particular if the beneficiaries are UK resident non doms and are subject to the arising basis of tax they'll be caught within this provision just as for UK domiciliaries.

So a non dom looking to make use of an offshore trust for capital gains tax avoidance would need to ensure that this beneficiaries charge did not apply.

This could be achieved by ensuring that:

- There were no UK resident beneficiaries, or
- There were no capital payments made to UK resident ,non dom beneficiaries who were subject to the arising basis.
- Any capital payments made to UK resident, non dom beneficiaries claiming the remittance basis were retained overseas (even if the trust assets sold were UK assets).
- Provided this was the case, the gains would be free of tax in the trust (assuming the assets were not UK business assets).

Chapter 27

How Non Doms Can Remit Income & Gains Tax Free With Offshore Trusts

In this chapter we'll look at some of the sundry tax planning techniques for non doms to avoid tax by using offshore trusts.

Offshore trusts

Offshore trusts can still be an effective shelter for capital gains providing the gains aren't remitted.

There are various methods by which offshore trusts can realise capital gains and UK beneficiaries could still benefit. For instance:

Washing out gains

Under this trustees could make a capital payment mopping up 'trust gains' to either a:

- non-UK domiciled beneficiary (claiming the remittance basis) outside the UK who does not remit the gains or a
- non- UK resident beneficiary

There is therefore no taxable gain charged on the beneficiary.

In the following year a capital payment is made either to a UK domiciled beneficiary or to a non-UK domiciled beneficiary who remits the payment to the UK. While such a payment could be matched with future trust gains, the Year 1 trust gains effectively escape UK CGT provided the first beneficiary does not remit the payment.

TAX PLANNING WITH OFFSHORE COMPANIES & TRUSTS | 133

Rolling up capital payments

If the trust is making a number of disposals it makes sense for the trust to realise capital gains over several years then make one capital distribution to non dom beneficiaries.

This way they only need to pay one £30,000/£50,000 to claim the remittance basis.

Drip feeding income or gains

The trust could drip feed foreign income or gains of less than £2,000 to UK resident, non domiciled beneficiaries.

Provided the beneficiaries' total unremitted income or gains is less than £2,000, the remittance basis applies automatically and there is no loss of allowances/requirement to pay £30,000/£50,000.

Using Parallel trusts

One of the problems with washing out gains (explained above) is that future gains can be allocated to the capital payments. One way around this is to use parallel trusts so that future gains arise in a separate trust.

Using loans to avoid capital payments

UK residents are allocated gains where they receive capital payments. However if a non-UK domiciled beneficiary lends money to the trustees of a non-UK settlement, repayment by the trustees is not a capital payment. Therefore this could be useful in avoiding tax on trust gains.

Example of tax planning using an offshore trust for non doms

Here's an example of the kind of planning that could be undertaken to allow a non dom to receive a capital sum from a trust without also being charged to CGT.

Albert is UK resident but non UK domiciled.

He owns an overseas property currently showing a gain of £500,000.

Albert borrows £500,000 secured over the property.

He creates an offshore trust and lends or gifts the borrowed funds to the new trust.

The trust buys the property from Albert at open market value (£500,000) using the borrowed funds.

The following year the trust disposes of the property for £500,000.

Albert could use other overseas funds to settle the debt and can now draw down from the trust a capital payment which does not have any gains allocated to it.

UK investments via trusts

It's worthwhile noting that if you have an offshore company selling assets at a gain the UK shareholder (owning more than 10%) would be taxed if the gains were remitted by the company (being a 'relevant person'), even if the gains were not received by the shareholder.

By contrast, where the gain was realised within a trust, the trustees could reinvest in the UK without there necessarily being a tax penalty for the beneficiaries.

Therefore offshore trusts are potentially more flexible than offshore companies in terms of capital gains avoidance.

Chapter 28

Advanced Tax Planning For Non Doms Using Offshore Trusts To Purchase UK Property

Here's one idea for some advanced tax planning for non doms looking to remit offshore income gains into the UK free of UK tax.

Scenario:

You have a non dom with substantial unremitted income or capital gains. They want to bring cash into the UK to acquire a UK property but avoid inheritance tax.

They could of course use an offshore company but this would create problems in terms of the non dom occupying the property (as there could be benefit in kind/income tax implications with the use of the property at less than market rent).

One option to use the offshore funds to acquire a UK property directly in their own name, whilst avoiding many of the anti avoidance rules is as follows:

- They acquire shares in an offshore company containing an offshore asset.

- The shares in the offshore company are transferred to an offshore trust which has the non dom as a beneficiary for life. The transfer of the shares would be a disposal but as the non dom is claiming the remittance basis there is no CGT charge. Note that we therefore assume the non dom is paying the £30,000 tax charge.

- The offshore company sells the asset. This would be a disposal for CGT purposes but as the company is non-resident there would be no CGT charge.

- The non dom is claiming the remittance basis and paying the £30,000 tax charge and therefore there would be no tax charge under the anti avoidance rules.

- The offshore company then loans the proceeds from the sale to the offshore trust on an arm's length basis (i.e. interest is payable from the offshore trust to the company).

- The non dom then borrows the proceeds from the Trust interest-free and uses them to buy a house; they have charged the house to the Trust, which has charged the debt to the company.

- Each year, the Trustee waives its right to a dividend, in consideration for which the company waives its right to interest.

So you have a net position where the non dom owns the property in their own name. Although the property would fall within their UK estate for inheritance tax purposes the loan to the offshore trust would reduce the value of their estate.

On a future disposal of the property they'd be able to qualify for principal private residence relief to eliminate the capital gain.

Of course if the non dom had left the UK prior to the disposal the capital gain would be free of UK CGT in any case.

Clearly this kind of planning would only be undertaken by someone with substantial resources given you'd need to establish the various entities and ensure they were non-resident as well as the other set up costs of such a structure.

Chapter 29

UK Domiciliaries And Offshore Trusts

We're often asked about when an offshore trust can be used tax efficiently. As we've see in the last few chapters it can be very attractive for non domiciliaries - but what about UK domiciliaries? In this chapter we look at when offshore trusts can be used by UK and how they are taxed in the UK.

Using an offshore trust involves a number of UK anti avoidance rules.

Firstly to establish the trust as non- resident you would need to ensure that all of the trustees were non- resident.

If you establish a trust as non-resident there are a variety of potential UK tax advantages, however the benefits will be heavily restricted. We'll look at the UK tax implications below

Inheritance tax

The transfer to a UK discretionary trust would usually be a chargeable lifetime transfer, and the trust itself would be subject to the inheritance tax regime for discretionary trusts. As such there would be a 10 year anniversary charge and an exit charge on the distribution of assets from the trust.

However providing the settlor survives for 7 years from the date of the transfer the assets transferred would usually be excluded from their estate for IHT purposes.

If you used an offshore trust, the inheritance tax implications would be similar. The transfer to the trust would be a chargeable lifetime transfer ('CLT') for IHT purposes, and therefore a transfer of value above your remaining nil rate band would be subject to a lifetime IHT charge. If the trust was a non-resident trust you would not be able to defer gains on the transfer to the trust.

If the trust was an excluded property trust it would be outside the scope of the UK IHT discretionary trust regime.

However in order for it to be an excluded property trust it would need to hold non UK assets and be established by a non UK domiciliary. If you are a UK domiciliary the trust would therefore be subject to the usual regime of 10 yearly anniversary charges and exit charges.

Capital Gains Tax

The non-resident trust would be outside the scope of UK CGT, unless it held assets used in a UK trade. In addition it would be likely there would be no CGT levied in the overseas jurisdiction where the trust is resident. This gives the offshore trust a clear advantage over a UK trust.

However there are two key anti avoidance rules that can apply.

Firstly, S86 TCGA 1992 which attributes gains of an offshore trust to UK resident settlors if defined people are actual or potential beneficiaries or receive a benefit.

The term "defined person" includes the settlor/their spouse, their children and their children's spouses and their grandchildren and their grandchildren's spouses.

This is a very wide anti avoidance rule and means that an offshore trust could only be used to shelter gains if your spouse, children and grandchildren (and their respective spouses) were all totally excluded from benefiting from the trust.

If they weren't then the settlor would be taxed on the gains of the trust during their lifetime.

In the future after they were deceased the gains would effectively be taxed on distributions to the beneficiaries (see below).

Income

As a non-resident trust it would be exempt from UK income tax on foreign income. Therefore by retaining trust income producing investments overseas the trust could avoid a UK income tax liability.

There are provisions to attribute income to UK individuals if they transfer assets to an offshore trust and have the power to enjoy or benefit from the trust. Therefore in order for the settlor to avoid being taxed directly on the income of the trust they would need to ensure that they and their spouse were totally excluded from benefiting from the trust.

If the trust beneficiaries were UK resident children and grandchildren, the trust could therefore initially operate as an effective shelter for foreign income. On the settlor's death it could then become a CGT shelter.

It should be noted that a distribution to the UK beneficiaries would be subject to UK income tax.

However the scope of the tax charge would vary.

Chapter 30

Using Offshore Trusts To Purchase Property

Using offshore trusts to purchase property (both in the UK and overseas) is very popular. There can in certain cases be significant tax advantages from this type of planning.

Using an offshore trust to buy a UK property to reduce UK tax

'Can I use an offshore trust to buy a UK property and save UK tax?' - It's a common question that we're asked, particularly by non doms who may already have an offshore structure in place.

In this chapter we look at the key UK tax implications of using an offshore trust to purchase a UK property.

Capital Gains Tax

One of the big motives for using an offshore trust is to avoid capital gains tax on a disposal of the property in the future.

If you owned a UK property personally you'd be potentially subject to CGT on a future disposal. Even if you were a non dom and claimed the remittance basis you'd be subject to CGT given that the property is in the UK.

If you used an offshore trust to hold the property, it would be exempt from CGT if it's classed as non UK resident. So the advantage is pretty clear.

It's not quite as simple as this though, as there are the various anti avoidance rules that can apply.

It's worth noting that as from April 2013 offshore (non-resident) companies will be subject to UK CGT on the disposal of UK residential property if the property is valued at more than £2Million.

TAX PLANNING WITH OFFSHORE COMPANIES & TRUSTS | 141

That's not all. Such properties will also be subject to an annual charge based on the property value.

This will be as follows:

Property Value Proposed Annual Charge

Property Value	Proposed Annual Charge
£2m to £5m	£15,000
£5m to £10m	£35,000
£10m to £20m	£70,000
Over £20m	£140,000

However, offshore trusts are specifically excluded from these provisions.

Even if your property is valued at less than £2 Million or is held by an offshore trust there are other general provisions if you're UK resident to tax any gain that arises to the offshore trust on you.

If you're a UK domiciliary you will be taxed on any gains that the trust realises. This doesn't apply though if you're a non UK domiciliary as the 2008 Finance Act preserved the exception for non UK domiciliaries.

There is a separate set of provisions that applies to tax the gains of offshore trusts on beneficiaries.

These apply where 'capital payments' are paid from the trust to you. In this case the amounts that you receive from the trust can be treated as gains. So if for instance the trust realises gains of £1,000,000 and makes capital payments to UK resident beneficiaries of £2,000,000; £1,000,000 of the receipts would be potentially taxable under the deemed capital gains rules.

So UK resident beneficiaries would only usually see benefits from using an offshore trust if there were no capital payments made -- at least while they were UK resident. The capital gains are only attributed to UK residents so the offshore trust could simply hold the proceeds abroad and distribute the proceeds after the beneficiaries were non UK resident to avoid any CGT charge.

The beneficiaries would need to ensure that they were non-resident for at least 5 tax years to avoid the deemed gain from the offshore trust being taxed in the year of their return.

Non UK domiciliaries have a further advantage when it comes to offshore trusts as the capital payments rules that apply to non doms won't apply where the remittance basis is claimed -- even though the offshore trust owns a UK property (unlike the rest of the anti avoidance rules).

Of course you would need to be either resident in the UK for less than 8 tax years or pay the £30,000 tax charge (rising to £50,000 for more than 12 years of UK residence) to benefit from this, but where it does apply the non doms could secure a CGT saving by simply reinvesting the proceeds that were extracted from the offshore trust overseas.

Income tax

If you use an offshore trust to purchase the property, and provided the trust is non-resident then the rental income would be subject to the non-resident landlord scheme. As such, basic rate income tax would be deducted from the rental income at source, or alternatively the trust could look at filing a claim to receive the rental income gross, without UK tax being deducted.

Note that any interest that was incurred by the offshore entity in purchasing the property could be deducted if the rental income was accounted for via a UK tax return.

So unlike the general CGT exemption for properties the trust itself could be within the scope of UK tax on the any rental income.

There are, though, still anti avoidance rules that can tax the income on you personally.

As we've seen in previous chapters the legislation imposes an income tax liability on individuals ordinarily resident in the UK in three broad circumstances:-

- under section 720 ITA, where they have power to enjoy income which arises to an offshore trust where the income arises as a result of a transfer of assets and/or associated operations;

- under section 727, where they receive or are entitled to receive capital sums as a result of a transfer of assets and/or associated operations, which have resulted in income arising to an offshore trust;

- under section 731, where they receive a benefit provided out of assets available for the purpose as a result of a transfer of assets and/or associated operations, which have resulted in income arising to an offshore trust.

Therefore anyone who established an offshore trust and transferred assets to it could easily find themselves taxed on any income arising if they can derive a benefit from the trust.

There is a key exception to this if the trust was established without a tax avoidance motive.

These transfer of asset provisions also apply to non UK domiciliaries albeit in an amended form. The broad aim is to tax them on the same basis as if they'd owned the assets personally and therefore if they are entitled to use the remittance basis of tax (in other words if they either make a claim or are entitled due to the £2,000 de minimis limit for unremitted overseas income and gains) they are subject to the remittance basis on the offshore trust income.

Essentially, therefore, if the offshore trust income is non UK income it would be subject to the remittance basis and provided it was not remitted by the settlor (or any benefits etc. weren't received in the UK) there should be no UK tax on the settlor.

If the asset owned by the offshore trust was a UK asset the remittance basis wouldn't apply and the non dom would be taxed on the trust income whether retained overseas or not.

So in the case of a UK property that was owned directly by an offshore trust, non doms wouldn't gain any benefit from the remittance basis in terms of rental income. The income of the trust could still be taxed on you in the UK.

Note though that you'd be allowed the same deductions and reliefs as if the income had been yours and therefore interest etc. could be offset. In addition, basic rate tax is avoided where the income has already suffered basic rate tax (e.g. under the non-resident landlord scheme).

If the UK property had been owned by an offshore company the trust would then be treated as owning an overseas asset (i.e. the shares in the overseas company).

However this wouldn't provide significant income tax benefits as the company would still be subject to the non-resident landlord scheme.

The trust income could be subject to the remittance basis on you to ensure you don't suffer a personal UK tax charge provided you retained the income overseas.

Inheritance tax

As the trust owns UK property this wouldn't constitute excluded property for UK tax purposes. Therefore the trust (even though offshore) would potentially be subject to the UK inheritance tax regime that applies to discretionary trusts (10 yearly charges and exit charges etc). The nil rate band could still be taken into account though.

If you used an offshore company to hold the UK property, with the shares in the property then held by the offshore trust this would ensure that the UK property was completely outside the scope of UK inheritance tax (as the non-resident trust would then be treated as owning an overseas asset) provided you were non domiciled when the trust was set up.

TAX PLANNING WITH OFFSHORE COMPANIES & TRUSTS | 145

Buy personally or via a UK company?

The other options are to use either a UK company or to hold personally.

Holding personally can have significant advantages where you're looking at leaving the UK in the future. This will enable you to avoid CGT, but you'd just have the income tax charge. If you have a highly leveraged purchase the interest could reduce the taxable rental significantly (although less so in the current climate).

The property would still be within your UK estate for inheritance tax purposes, although you could split ownership and use multiple nil rate bands to reduce the taxable sum.

Even if you used an offshore trust, though, you'd still suffer income tax on the rental income, and the anti avoidance rules would be in point.

Using UK company is generally the worst option:

- There is no scope for avoiding CGT with non-residence
- There is the potential double tax charge in the company

It would therefore only be in limited circumstances (e.g. to utilise capital losses etc.) that using a company would be preferable.

Chapter 31

Getting Money Out of Offshore Trusts Tax Efficiently

If you receive cash from an offshore trust you need to know what UK tax will be due on the receipts.

For UK residents they'll need to decide whether there is a liability to income tax or capital gains tax.

UK resident, UK domiciliaries are charged to income tax on their worldwide income. Therefore any income receipts from an offshore trust will be taxed as UK income, and subject to the standard rates of income tax.

If however, the amounts are gifts of capital, the capital gains tax rules will need to be considered.

First, there are provisions that can treat capital benefits received from an offshore trust as income. This would therefore subject the capital receipts to income tax. As well as cash transfers, this could also apply to other benefits such as an interest free loan or free use of accommodation provided by the offshore trust.

There are two main 'exemptions' from this charge to income tax.

Firstly, there is an exemption if the trust was not established for UK tax planning reasons and if there was a genuine commercial motive.

This could be the case where a trust was established by a beneficiary's relative a number of years ago and there was clearly no UK tax planning motive.

Secondly, the income charge only applies where there is relevant income in the trust. In other words the trust needs to have income that is capable of distributing to beneficiaries. If there is no such income then there is no benefit taxed as income under this section.

If this section doesn't apply there is an alternative tax charge though and this is under capital gains tax.

Capital payments from the trust to beneficiaries are charged as capital gains provided the trust has actually realised capital gains.

For this to apply, the trust needs to have realised capital gains. Therefore the trustees need to keep track of what gains have been realised (based on UK rules) and allocate them to capital payments to beneficiaries.

The combination of the two provisions mean that trust income or capital gains could be used to establish a tax charge on UK beneficiaries receiving cash from offshore trusts if the trust had realised income or capital gains. If there were neither, capital receipts could be free of tax.

By far the best way to extract cash from an offshore trust is as a non UK resident. As a non- resident it's possible to extract cash from the trust free of UK income and capital gains tax.

If you are subject to UK tax on any receipt from an offshore trust, ensure that you take detailed advice on it, and very importantly - obtain full details of the trusts income and gains from the trustees.

How distributions from offshore trusts to UK residents are taxed

Beneficiaries of offshore trusts will be looking at how to extract cash from the trust tax efficiently. Broadly speaking there are two options:

- Income distribution

- Capital distribution

Income distributions

Distributions of income to a UK beneficiary are subject to UK income tax. If the beneficiary is a non UK domiciliary and is subject to the remittance basis they could avoid income tax by retaining the cash overseas. For most non doms using the remittance basis would mean losing the benefit of the

UK allowances and also raise the spectre of the £30,000/£50,000 remittance basis charge.

It's worth noting that if the beneficiary is also the trust settlor special rules apply to tax the income and gains on the settlor directly.

Capital distributions

Capital distributions from an offshore trust will be taxed under the anti avoidance rules. There are two sets of rules that could apply.

Firstly there's the transfer of asset provisions that can apply to tax capital distributions as income where there is accumulated 'relevant' income in the trust or underlying company.

If there is no relevant income in the trust or if the motive exemption applied there would be no tax charge under this provision. However, in this case the beneficiary would be subject to CGT if there are capital gains in the trust.

The capital gains tax charge on the beneficiary effectively looks to tax capital gains that have arisen to the trust (but were exempt as it's non-resident) on the beneficiary. There would need to be a separate pool to match the gains with capital payments to beneficiaries. The gains are only allocated to capital payments once.

Non Doms

Non Doms who use the remittance basis can also be taxed on the remittance basis on the distribution from the trust. This means that although the anti avoidance rules above can apply to tax the distribution to either income tax or CGT, if the cash is retained abroad no UK tax charge would arise.

Why make an income distribution?

Lots of offshore trusts distribute trust income as income.

This has some advantages including:

- Withholding tax borne by the income is set against UK tax charged on the beneficiary
- The income could be directed at low or nil income beneficiaries (e.g. children)
- UK tax is avoided if the beneficiary is non-resident or non domiciled and claims the remittance basis (and retains the income abroad).

Complexity of capital distributions

Capital distributions can be very complex. It is essential that the trustees provide a full computation of their income and gains for each year. It is necessary to know the total since inception of the trust less any previously allocated to income or capital payments.

If there is no relevant income or capital gains in the trust there would be no tax on the receipt, at least at the date of the payment. If relevant income or capital gains arose in the future a tax charge could well apply in the future.

An option to avoid a future tax charge would be to distribute all of the trust (or resettle after the tax year of the distribution).

Distribute to a non-resident or non dom

A good solution is to distribute the trust fund to a non-resident or a non dom beneficiary.

Distributions to non-residents are free of CGT (provided they have satisfied any 5 year anti avoidance requirements). Non dom beneficiaries could also be free of CGT if they use the remittance basis of tax and retain the cash overseas.

The trustees could therefore eliminate any tax issues by distributing to non-residents or non doms.

The same could also be true if they distributed an amount equal to the net trust gains to date to non-residents. In this case the trustees could then distribute the rest of the trust fund free of tax to UK beneficiaries the following year. This works because the distribution to non- residents is still classed as a distribution for the purposes of allocating capital payments.

Therefore it could wash out the capital gains to date leaving a capital payment to UK resident beneficiaries with no gains to allocate.

It's important for this strategy that the capital payment to the UK beneficiaries is in the next tax year otherwise HMRC will just allocate the trust gains on a pro rate basis between the UK resident and non-resident capital payment.

It may then be advisable to wind up the trust or resettle any assets to prevent future gains being allocated to the payments.

Splitting the trust

Another option could be to consider splitting the trust with the amount of any potential capital payment being settled in the new trust. The distribution could then be made in the new tax year from the new trust. The benefit of this is that only a proportionate part of the trust gains would be transferred to the new trusts and therefore only part of the gains would be allocated to the capital payment under S87.

Where you're caught by the income tax rules

If you're caught by the income tax anti avoidance rules in the transfer of asset provisions (as above) any capital payments to non- residents are tax free but they don't 'wash out' the relevant income. This means that it won't reduce the amount of relevant income taxable in the UK and therefore the strategy above of distributing an amount equivalent to the trust income to non-residents wouldn't then allow a tax free capital payment to UK resident beneficiaries.

Distribute income to avoid the avoidance rules?

Whilst you can't use capital payments to wash out the relevant income in the offshore trust you could always simply make regular payments out of income to a non- resident or non dom beneficiary. This would be tax free (subject to the remittance basis for the non dom) but would also reduce the relevant income.

It may therefore be possible to 'wash out' the relevant income this way by making actual distributions.

Chapter 32

Q & A's On Offshore Trusts

Transfer of property from offshore trust to UK beneficiary

Question:

A non UK Domiciled Trust, Settled by a Non UK/Tax resident person owns a property in the UK. Can this Trust gift the property to a UK Domiciled/Tax Resident beneficiary free of CGT? The property is empty and not rented out, and used occasionally (say twice a year) for the benefit of the Settlor on visits to the UK.

Answer:

There are a few issues to consider here. The transfer of the property would be free of CGT in the hands of the trust for 2013/2014, as it's non-resident, and the property is not used for the purposes of a UK trade.

You'd also need to look at the impact of the anti avoidance rules to assess the extent to which there could be a tax charge on the beneficiary (given there could be no UK tax charge on the beneficiary if he's non UK resident).

The first issue would be the transfer of asset rules which could apply given this applies to the transfer of assets in specie. If there is undistributed 'relevant income' in the trust this could ensure that an income tax charge applied on the benefit received by the beneficiary. Note that there is a motive exemption to potentially exclude this.

The other issue is the application of the capital payments rules.

The capital payments rules include the transfer of assets in specie and therefore this would be classed as a capital payment, representing the value of the property transferred. If there were any unallocated gains of the trust they could be treated as arising on the UK beneficiary up to the amount of capital payment received.

Using an offshore trust to hold Italian property

Tax Question:

Dear Sirs,

A person not UK Deemed domiciled would like to pass her Italian property to her son avoiding or reducing the impact of UK IHT.

Could a Discretionary Trust do the trick? Given that the property is an excluded property and she is not deemed domiciled yet, there would not be any charge in putting the Italian asset into the Trust. Is it correct to say that if the Trust is offshore, no 10 year charge and no exit charge will be due on a structure like this?

Do you see any other possible downside?

many thanks

Answer:

Yes, if she's not UK domiciled or deemed domiciled yet, (but may be in the future) using an offshore trust would be beneficial. The trust would be an excluded property trust and exempt from the UK IHT regime of periodic and exit charges. It is her domicile at the date of transfer that is crucial to determine the trust's tax treatment - not the fact that she may become UK deemed domiciled in the future.

The transfer of the property into the trust would be a disposal for CGT purposes but if she is claiming the remittance basis (or some other relief such as PPR relief applies) she should be able to avoid CGT on the transfer.

Any disposal of the property by the trust would not be taxed on the Mother as the provisions that attribute gains to UK settlors don't apply to non doms.

Attribution of capital gains of offshore trust to UK beneficiaries

Tax Question:

If a Trust is set up by a non dom for the benefit of his children who are residents of UK, when the proceeds are distributed can the Trust offset the gains from the losses before paying the capital gains tax or is it to be treated like an individual non-dom and not allowed to use any losses ?

Answer:

I assume you're referring to the rules that tax UK residents on the gains of offshore trusts when capital payments are made? In that case the capital losses should be available for offset against the trust gains before there is an attribution of the gain to the UK beneficiaries.

Use of a trust by non-residents prior to a return to UK residence

Tax Question:

Trusts.

I have read with great interest quite a lot of your excellent books but am not clever enough to see if there is a practical answer to the following. Husband and wife both UK domiciled , non-resident many years considering returning to UK.

Are there any practical steps that can be taken whilst non-resident to reduce the impact of UK tax once they return ?

It would appear that the use of a trust would cause further problems and tax. Please could you give your advice ? Thank you

Answer:

It depends on the particular circumstances.

In terms of capital gains tax, for instance, it can make sense for them to crystallise capital gains whilst non-resident. This can be achieved by a transfer to a connected party such as a company or trust prior to their return/prior to the tax year of return.

In terms of tax on income there could be an advantage in using an offshore trust to shelter foreign income.

The trust would need to be established as non-resident (with foreign trustees etc.). The big problem with using an offshore trust in this way is the transfer of asset provisions. These can attribute income of the offshore trusts to UK residents who have transferred assets into the trust. This income would then be taxed in the UK.

However, there is an exemption where the transfer was for commercial purposes or there was no UK tax avoidance motive. One of the key occasions when it can apply is where non-residents transfer assets into trusts for the purposes of overseas tax planning.

If it could be demonstrated that this applied, when the non-residents subsequently became UK resident the offshore trust income shouldn't be taxed in the UK until there was a trust distribution.

Additions to NZ trust to avoid IHT?

Tax Question:

I hold a NZ family trust and am considering purchasing a property in the UK. This was established when I was not domiciled in the UK but I am now domiciled here.

I understand that UK property will therefore not meet excluded property status and therefore be liable to IHT (unlike NZ property).

It has been suggested that I hold any UK property in a NZ overseas company to maintain excluded property status and legally avoid IHT. Would this overseas company need to be in place prior to any purchase of UK assets by the NZ trust or could the NZ trust purchase UK assets as it currently stands and then be restructured in NZ without incurring UK IHT liability as a result of the temporary holding of the UK property in the NZ trust?

Answer:

The trust qualifies for excluded property status to the the extent that it held foreign property whilst you were non UK domiciled. The fact that you have acquired a UK domicile would not impact on the IHT treatment of any foreign property held in the trust and this would therefore be outside the UK IHT regime for trusts.

However, after you have acquired a UK domicile you could not then add property to the trust and benefit from the excluded property status. The purchase of any foreign property by the trust (i.e. additions of foreign property to the trust by you) would be within the scope of UK IHT for the trust.

Therefore if you purchased UK property this would clearly be subject to the UK IHT regime for trusts. However, so would any foreign property (such as shares in an offshore company owning the UK property) given you are now a UK domiciliary.

Tax on receipt from offshore trust

Question:

1. I am a non-dom who will be using the remittance basis and paying the £30,000.

2. I receive income distributions from two trusts which I plan to keep abroad (and to pay the £30,000) -- I understand that if I remitted this, it would be taxed as income.

3. Should I want to have a capital disbursement made from the trust and remitted to the UK, would the income payment be ignored as this is kept abroad and what level of tax would I be required to pay?

4. Apart from the inheritance tax advantages of a trust, are there any

TAX PLANNING WITH OFFSHORE COMPANIES & TRUSTS | 157

other advantages to keeping the monies in a trust or would it make sense to disband this and have separate capital / capital gains / income accounts so that 'pure' capital could be remitted to the UK in the future?

I look forward to hearing from you.

Answer:

Distributions of income to a UK beneficiary are subject to UK income tax. Therefore if you were a non UK domiciliary and was subject to the remittance basis you could avoid income tax by retaining the cash overseas.

Capital distributions from an offshore trust will be taxed under the anti avoidance rules.

There are two sets of rules that could apply.

Firstly there's the transfer of asset provisions that can apply to tax capital distributions as income where there is accumulated 'relevant' income in the trust or underlying company.

'Relevant' income for this purpose means income that arises to the offshore trust or company which can be used to provide a benefit for the beneficiary concerned. Income is only taken into account once for this purpose. Therefore rental income for instance received by the trust and held in the trust would be treated as relevant income for this purposes.

If there is any relevant income in the trust and a capital distribution is made the capital distribution could be taxed on the UK resident beneficiary as income to the extent of the relevant income.

This is subject to the motive exemption.

If there is no relevant income in the trust or if the motive exemption applied there would be no tax charge under this provision. However, in this case the beneficiary would be subject to CGT if there are capital gains in the trust.

The capital gains tax charge on the beneficiary effectively looks to tax capital gains that have arisen to the trust (but were exempt as it's non-resident) on the beneficiary. There would need to be a separate pool to match the gains with capital payments to beneficiaries. The gains are only allocated to capital payments once.

Non Doms who use the remittance basis can also be taxed on the remittance basis on the capital distribution from the trust. This means that although the anti avoidance rules above can apply to tax the distribution to either income tax or CGT, if the cash is retained abroad no UK tax charge would arise.

In terms of disbanding the trust you should ensure that this is considered in detail. However, as you state, the key advantages would be in terms of inheritance tax if the trust is an excluded property trust.

It could be advantageous to distribute the overseas trust assets to you as non dom where you are subject to the remittance basis. You would however need to keep the receipts abroad to avoid tax. In terms of your other overseas assets you could, as you state, use separate capital/income etc. accounts to remit any clean capital back to the UK.

Providing you're subject to the remittance basis, though, the trust would not have any income tax/CGT advantages as you'd be taxed on the remittance basis on any overseas income/capital gains in any case.

Investing and shares and ETFs via an offshore trust

Question:

I am UK resident but non UK domiciled and have an offshore trust which has substantial cash assets. I am looking at investing some of the funds into shares via an exchange traded fund ('ETF').

I want to understand the UK tax implications of these investments for any income that is generated. Does is matter where I invest the cash (e.g. US/UK or Europe)?

TAX PLANNING WITH OFFSHORE COMPANIES & TRUSTS | 159

Answer:

On the assumption that the trust is non UK resident, there is a general rule that the tax charged on most types of investment income including dividends from investments is limited to the tax, if any, deducted at source.

However, this limitation does not apply to non-resident trusts if a current or potential beneficiary is a UK ordinarily resident individual. As such the offshore trust would be charged to UK income tax on UK investment income. Providing the income generated was offshore income, a non resident trust would however not be charged to UK tax. It would be necessary to consider the source of the income. A UK incorporated company would be classed as a UK source, as would any company traded in a UK exchange. Therefore in order for the offshore trust to be exempt from UK income tax it would need to invest in funds that were not traded in a UK market.

You would need to be careful as to the extent of any anti avoidance provisions that could apply here. In particular there are provisions that could apply where a UK ordinarily resident individual transfers assets overseas (e.g. cash to an offshore trust) and could make the income taxable on the UK settlor.

Although you're a non UK domiciliary these provisions can still impact on you, particularly as regards income of the trust if you are not claiming the remittance basis of tax.

Tax questions on using an offshore trust

Tax Question:

What are the benefits (CGT, IHT, Income Tax) of an offshore trust created & initially settled by a UK citizen whilst non-dom, who returns to the UK either by choice, or by illness? The beneficiaries of the Trust are the settlor's children & remoter children.

1. What is the difference if the settlors are also beneficiaries?

2. Can the settlors settle more money into the Trust whilst UK resident?

3. Would loans at any stage by the settlors to the Trust or vice versa mitigate tax?

4. The Trust is for asset protection -- how can it be proved "the trust was established without a tax avoidance motive"? 5. What difference would it make if HMRC many years down the line did not agree that the settlors were Non-dom when the Trust was created & initially settled ?

Answer:

In terms of the benefits, then the trust would be an excluded property trust for tax purposes. As such the foreign assets of the trust would be outside the scope of UK IHT. The trust itself would be exempt from CGT so long as it didn't hold property valued at more than £2Million and the settlors wouldn't be attributed gains of the trust if they were non doms. The trust would also be outside the scope of UK income tax on foreign income.

Providing the settlors and spouse/minor children couldn't benefit from the trust they shouldn't be taxed on the income of the trust. The beneficiaries would be taxed on trust distributions.

In terms of your questions:

1. What is the difference if the settlors are also beneficiaries?

   The settlors are taxed on gains of the trust. However beneficiaries can be taxed on trust gains if they receive capital payments/benefits from the trust. Therefore the settlors could be subject to CGT on distributions.

   Also if the settlors are beneficiaries they would have the power to enjoy trust assets and they would need to consider the transfer of asset provisions which could tax them on trust income (unless there was no UK tax avoidance motive).

2. Can the settlors settle more money into the Trust whilst UK resident?

Yes they could do, but this would bring into play the transfer of asset rules.

3. Would loans at any stage by the settlors to the Trust or vice versa mitigate tax?

This is unlikely.

4. The Trust is for asset protection -- how can it be proved "the trust was established without a tax avoidance motive"?

You'd need to provide clear reasons for the creation of trust and ensure that these were all supported by the relevant documentary evidence (e.g. advice letters etc.) that showed the asset protection motive.

5. What difference would it make if HMRC many years down the line did not agree that the settlors were Non-dom when the Trust was created & initially settled ?

Then the trust wouldn't get the benefit of the IHT exemptions

Loans from Offshore Trust to UK Doms

Question:

How can Loans from Offshore Trusts to UK doms be structured and planned?

1. Can loans be made for the life of the trust (e.g. up to 100 years)?

2. Can loans be repaid from a UK estate (e.g. on death), and are they then deductible from UK IHT?

3. Do loans have to bear interest? If so, how much?

4. Are there any other tax implications?

Thank you

Answer:

There are a lot of issues when considering loans from offshore trusts to UK resident and domiciled individuals.

Loans can be made for the life of the trust and also do not have to bear interest. However one issue that would need to be borne in mind would be the anti avoidance rules. The transfer of asset provisions can tax individuals who receive benefits from an offshore trust. This does not need to be the settlor of the trust and the beneficiary will frequently be another individual.

Receiving a benefit from the trust is given a wide scope and can include a loan at below market interest rates. Therefore in the case of an interest free loan to a UK resident the provisions could apply to treat the UK resident as receiving taxable income equivalent to the interest saved (based on the market interest rate).

There are a number of exceptions and caveats to this including:

It won't apply if the motive defence applied. A common application of this could be where the trust was established for non UK tax planning reasons by other non-resident family members. In this case there is no taxable benefit on the UK resident for the interest free loan.

The benefit is only taxed to the extent that the trust has 'relevant income' which is essentially trust income to be used for the beneficiaries. If the trust has no or limited income (e.g. only capital receipts) the benefit may not be taxed in any case.

Another issue would be that if the source of the loan was in the UK (e.g. secured over UK property and made to UK residents) the tax deduction at source provisions may apply to require basic rate tax at source to be deducted.

This would need to be reviewed. If applicable a double tax treaty could be considered.

If the loan was made to a UK domiciliary and was a valid loan it would be deductible (as a liability) from their estate for inheritance tax purposes.

You'd therefore need to consider carefully the loan bearing in mind the purpose of the loan and the specific position of the trust.

Appendix I

UK Tax Treatment of Overseas Entities

ANGUILLA Partnership	Transparent
ARGENTINA Sociedad de responsibilidad limitada	Opaque
AUSTRIA KG Kommanditgesellschaft	Transparent
KEG Kommand Erwerbsgesellschaft	Transparent
GmbH & Co KG	Transparent
GmbH Gesellschaft mit Beschrankter Haftung	Opaque
AG Aktiengesellschaft	Opaque
BELGIUM SPRL Societe de privee a responsabilite	Opaque
SNC Societe en nom collectif	Transparent
SA Societe Anonyme	Opaque
NV Naamloze Vennootschap	Opaque
SCA Societe en commanditaire par actions	Opaque
CVA Commanditaire venootschap op aandelen	Opaque
BRAZIL Srl Sociedad por quotas de responabilidade	Opaque

CANADA Partnership and limited partnership	Transparent
CAYMAN ISLANDS Limited partnership	Transparent
CHILE SRL Sociedad de responsibilidad limitada	Transparent
CHINA WFOE Wholly Foreign Owned Entity	Opaque
CZECH REPUBLIC as Akciova spolecnost	Opaque
sro Spolecnost s rucenim omezenym	Opaque
EUROPEAN UNION SE Societas Europeas	Opaque
FINLAND Ky Kommandiittiyhtio	Transparent
Oy Osakeyhtio	Opaque
Ab Aktiebolag	Opaque
FRANCE GIE Groupement d'Interet economique	Transparent
SNC Societe en nom collectif	Transparent
SCI Societe civile immobiliere	Opaque
SCS Societe en commandite simple	Transparent
SP Societe en participation	Transparent
SARL Societe a responsabilite limitee	Opaque
FCPR Fonds Commun de Placement a risques	Transparent
SAS Societe par Actions Simplifiee	Opaque
SA Societe Anonyme	Opaque

GFA Groupement Foncier d'Agricole	Opaque
SC Societe Civile	Opaque
GERMANY Stille Gesellschaft	Opaque
KG Kommandit Gesellschaft	Transparent
OHG Offene Handelsgesellschaft	Transparent
GmbH & Co. KG	Transparent
AG Aktiengesellschaft	Opaque
GUERNSEY LP Limited Partnership	Transparent
PCC Protected Cell Company	Opaque
Open Ended Investment Company/ Limited Liability	Opaque
HUNGARY Kft Korlatolt felelossegu tarsasag	Opaque
Rt. Reszvenytarsasag	Opaque
ICELAND Hlutafelag	Opaque
IRELAND Limited Partnership	Transparent
Irish Investment Limited Partnership	Transparent
CCF Common Contractual Fund	Transparent
ITALY SpA Societa per Azioni	Opaque
JAPAN Goshi-Kaisha	Transparent
Gomei Kaisha	Transparent

TK Tokumei Kumiai	Transparent
Kabushikikaisha	Opaque
Yugen-kaisha	Opaque
JERSEY LLP Limited Liability Partnership	Opaque
KAZAKHSTAN LLC Limited Liability Company	Opaque
LIECHTENSTEIN Anstalt	Opaque
FCP Fonds commun de placement	Transparent
SA Societe anonyme	Opaque
SARL Societe a responsabilite limitee	Opaque
SJCAV Societe d'investment a capitale variable	Opaque
NETHERLANDS VOF Vennootschap Onder Firma	Transparent
CV Commanditaire Vennootschap	Transparent
NV Naamloze Vennootschap	Opaque
Maatschap	Transparent
Stichting	Transparent
Co-op Cooperatie	Transparent
NEW CALEDONIA SNC Societe en nom collectif	Transparent
NORWAY AS Alkjeselskap	Opaque
KS Kommandittselkap	Transparent

SA Sociedade Anonima	Opaque
RUSSIA Joint Venture under "Decree No.49"	Opaque
LLC Limited Liability Company	Opaque
SPAIN SC Sociedad Civila	Opaque
SA Sociedad Anonima	Opaque
Srl Sociedad de Responsabilidad Limitada	Opaque
SWEDEN AB Aktiebolag	Opaque
KB Kommanditbolag	Transparent
SWITZERLAND SS Societe Simple	Transparent
GmbH Gesellschaft mit beschrankter Haftung	Opaque
TURKEY AP Attorney Partnership	Transparent
AS Anonim Sirket	Opaque
Ltd/S Limited Sirket	Opaque
USA Limited Partnership	Transparent
LLC Limited Liability Company	Opaque
LLP Limited Liability Partnership	Transparent
MBT Massachusetts Business Trust	Transparent
S. Corporation	Opaque

Pay Less Tax!

… with help from www.WealthProtectionReport.co.uk

- **Tax Planning Techniques Of The Rich & Famous** - Essential reading for anyone who wants to use the same tax planning techniques as the most successful Entrepreneurs, large corporations and celebrities

- **Non Resident & Offshore Tax Planning** – Detailed analysis of non UK residence and the new Statutory Residence Test.

- **Tax Planning For Company Owners** – Essential reading for anyone owning a UK company. This book looks at the corporation tax and income tax planning opportunities.

- **The Worlds Best Tax Havens** – Analysis of low and nil-tax countries you can use to reduce your taxes. Also includes an analysis of international tax planning techniques available.

- **Tax Saving Tactics For Non Doms** – Tax planning for non UK domiciliaries

- **How To Avoid CGT In 2013/2014** – Top CGT planning techniques for 2013/2014

- **Asset Protection Handbook** – Looks at strategies to ringfence your assets in today's increasing litigious climate

- **Working Overseas Guide** – Comprehensive analysis of how you can save tax when working overseas

- **Double Tax Treaty Planning** – How you can use double tax treaties to reduce UK taxes

Printed in Great Britain
by Amazon